I0817546

AUTOMOBILI
LAMBORGHINI

TEXT BY

SIMONLUCA PINI

automobili Lamborghini

PAST, PRESENT, FUTURE

SCHIFFER PUBLISHING
4880 Lower Valley Road • Atglen, PA 19310

CONTENTS

AUTOMOBILI
LAMBORGHINI

PREFACE

Lamborghini has always been synonymous with innovation, avant-garde design, and uncompromising emotions. This book, celebrating our passion for excellence, is so much more than a simple annual report—it is an interactive exploration of the Lamborghini universe, enriched with exclusive content accessible via QR codes.

Through these pages, we review the history of the marque, from its foundation to the present day, telling the story through the voices of those who have helped construct the legend: engineers, designers, managers, and all those people who, with dedication and talent, have made Lamborghini a global icon.

Lending added value to this story is Simonluca Pini, an established journalist in the automotive field and a true enthusiast. He has driven most of the cars described in this book, and his point of view brings an authentic and involving touch capable of transmitting to the reader the emotion of experiencing a Lamborghini.

I would like to invite you to immerse yourselves in this unique experience and discover not only our remarkable past, but also the exciting future that awaits us.

Enjoy reading!

Stephan Winkelmann

WHY ANOTHER BOOK ABOUT LAMBORGHINI?

BY SIMONLUCA PINI

A number of books have been written about Lamborghini, from its origins through the more recent events. But what has been missing is one telling the year-by-year story of the marque, with previously unpublished illustrations and firsthand accounts from those present for the company's most important milestones. Enhancing the added value of the book you are looking at, several of the models described have been driven by the author on road and track, while much of the text has been written in the historic factory at Sant'Agata Bolognese. Moreover, a number of models are accompanied by a QR code to be read with your smartphone camera that gives access to exclusive video content placing you inside the cockpit of a Lamborghini and allowing you to listen to the unmistakable symphony of the engines built at Sant'Agata Bolognese. The list of models that have been tested ranges from icons of the past such as the legendary Miura, also presented in contemporary drawings, and the Temerario, a model powered by the new V8 plug-in hybrid engine.

Although this is a photographic book, we have sought to combine the beauty of the images with a journalistic approach to describing the events that have accompanied the company founded by Ferruccio Lamborghini in 1963. How have we done this? Thanks to the stories recounted by those personally involved in the historic changes, those with firsthand knowledge of the backstory, as in the case of the acquisition of the entire Emilia-based firm by Audi in 1998. Ample space has been devoted to styling, with original sketches by Mitja Borkert, Lamborghini's head of design since 2016, and to the secrets of the new V8 twin-turbo plug-in hybrid power unit revealed by the chief technical officer Rouven Mohr. We couldn't not take an in-depth look at Lamborghini Squadra Corse, the competition side of the firm that over the course of more than a decade has conquered an impressive list of victories and has participated in the legendary 24 Hours of Le Mans with the Lamborghini SC63. In addition to to the past and the present, great attention has also been paid to the future, beginning with an analysis of the Lanzador concept car that anticipates the future all-electric model scheduled for 2028 and an overview of the Cor Tauri industrial plan, with an exclusive interview with the CEO, Stephan Winkelmann. All this is united by a single common denominator: a passion for Lamborghini and the cars that for over sixty years have left the factory at Sant'Agata Bolognese.

FROM THE BIRTH OF LAMBORGHINI TO FERRUCCIO'S FAREWELL

1963/1972

AUTOMOBILI
LAMBORGHINI

FERRUCCIO LAMBORGHINI:
BEYOND THE LEGEND OF THE FERRARI DUEL

April 28, 1916: the date of birth of the Lamborghini legend. Not that of the cars, but of Ferruccio Lamborghini, the founder of the firm, who, from farming stock, proved capable of revolutionizing several sectors, not just that of high-performance sports cars. Born at Renazzo in the province of Ferrara, from a very young age he displayed a passion for mechanical engineering and the automotive world. In 1946, following military service at Rhodes, in Greece, where he had worked as a repair mechanic in the 50th Mixed Motorized Division, improving his knowledge of diesel engines, he opened his first workshop at Cento, in the province of Ferrara. After having recognized the needs of the surrounding area, the following year he produced the first Lamborghini tractor known as the "Carioca"; from an initial single example a week, by 1950 annual production had reached 200 units. All this developed in parallel with Ferruccio Lamborghini's entrepreneurial spirit, with the inauguration of the new factory at Cento and an exponential growth in the number of tractors sold year by year. Not just tractors, but also burners and conditioners with the founding of "La Lamborghini Bruciatori e Condizionatori." The secret was the fertile Italian economy in the postwar period known as the "economic miracle," but above all Lamborghini himself, a perfect embodiment of the concept of the "self-made man" whose success was the fruit of his own talent—talent that translated into the grasping of opportunities in advance, the ability to select the best staff, and the desire to improve year by year, always to the fore and becoming the finest possible "salesman" for his company, whether it was selling a tractor to a farmer or dealing with the journalistic greats. It was actually Ferruccio's success in the world of agricultural machinery, combined with a passion for speed and the tuning of cars, that was the seed from which in 1963 germinated the Lamborghini we know today. In a blend of truth and legend, it all started with a challenge to Enzo Ferrari, after Lamborghini's complaints about the mechanical qualities of the cars produced at Maranello. What is indisputable is the result obtained, with the name "Lamborghini" becoming a global synonym for speed and style made in Italy.

LAMBORGHINI

THE BIRTH OF THE LAMBORGHINI FACTORY

"You earn more making cars than tractors" A contemporary quote from Ferruccio Lamborghini that neatly summarizes the birth in 1963 of the company we all know today. Although Lamborghini's announcement of the ambitious car project to the management of the two companies associated with the production of tractors and burners in the second half of 1962 aroused a climate of veiled skepticism among the employees, the production plant was completed in record time in the autumn of 1963, on land bought at Sant'Agata Bolognese. The small town in the province of Bologna, just 16 kilometers (10 miles) from Maranello and 25 kilometers (15.5 miles) from Modena, had no idea it was to become a cult location for all car enthusiasts. Naturally, the choice of site was by no means casual: Ferruccio knew that the area was home to qualified engineers and staff who had worked and continued to work at Ferrari and Maserati. Just as he had done with his other companies, he drew from his competitors the best the market offered, thanks to the passion and vision for the future he was able to transmit and his ability to understand at a glance the personal and professional values of the people before him. As noted in an article in *Ruoteclassiche* from 1993, Lamborghini's recruitment strategy was tried and trusted and based on a simple but effective concept: "In this way there are no research expenses; I took the best men from the other companies. I am the first Japanese in history. I do not invent anything; I start out from where others have arrived.

For the first car I wanted a 12-cylinder because the best engine was that of the Ferrari; all it needed was a modification to the cylinder head design as it had just a single overhead camshaft. The best were those of the Alfa Romeo, with twin camshafts, and so we had an exceptional engine." The design and development were entrusted to the thirty-six-year-old engineer from Livorno, Giotto Bizzarrini, who had worked at Ferrari for four years, contributing to several models, including the 250 GT 2+2 and the GTO; the young engineer Giampaolo Dallara, just twenty-six years old but with experience as a designer at Maserati after already having spent time at Ferrari; and the engineer Paolo Stanzani. The factory at No. 12 Via Modena has, over the course of more than sixty years, become the spirit and image of the cars carrying the Lamborghini badge and one of the cornerstones of Italy's Motor Valley.

1963

LAMBORGHINI 350 GTV

THE FIRST CAR OFF THE LINE

1963

LAMBORGHINI 350 GT

THE FIRST PRODUCED IN SERIES

While the 350 GTV from 1963 has the honor of being the first car to carry the Lamborghini name, in 1964 the 350 GT was the first Lamborghini car to enter series production. It took the 350 GTV as its base, with several elements being modified and styled by Carrozzeria Touring rather than Franco Scaglione, who had been responsible for the 350 GTV design. This decision rendered the project less extreme, with the taut lines and pop-up headlights of the GTV giving way to softer forms and oval headlamps. The production car was 14 centimeters (5.5 inches) longer, for a total of slightly over 4.65 meters (15.25 feet), with the wheelbase being lengthened by around 10 centimeters (14 inches), an increase that together with a less accentuated roofline guaranteed a 2+1 cabin with a third central seat at the rear and a more capacious trunk. The car was fitted with a 3,464 cc (211.39 cu. in.) V12 engine derived from the one designed by Bizzarrini—who had left Lamborghini that year to set out on his own entrepreneurial adventure—and was heavily modified by Stanzani and Dallara to facilitate production and provide a smoother drive. The six carburetors were now horizontal rather than vertical, thereby reducing the height of the mechanical organs, a wet sump replaced the dry sump lubrication system, new cam profiles were adopted, and the power output was reduced from 360 cv (355 hp) at 8,000 rpm to 270 cv (266 hp), good for a maximum speed of 250 kph (155 mph). The power unit was matched with a five-speed ZF gearbox, a self-locking differential, and a braking system with four Girling discs. Given a vote of confidence by the automotive journalists of the day, the car was dynamically convincing thanks to features such as all-round independent suspension. The 350 GT went on sale in 1964 priced from 5,500,000 lire; it was also offered in a more powerful form developing 320 cv (315.5 hp) thanks to different cam profiling and a modified fuel system. Produced through early 1966, a total of 131 examples of the Lamborghini 350 GT were built, of which fewer than ten had the central rear seat.

1964

LAMBORGHINI 400 GT

THE FIRST 2+2

An evolution of the 350 GT, the Lamborghini 400 GT went into production in 1966 in two-seater coupé and 2+2 versions. Recognizable thanks to a series of modifications such as the twin circular rather than oval headlights and the new radiator grille, the 400 GT concealed its most interesting novelty under the large front hood. The V12 engine now displaced close to 4 liters (244 cu. in.); hence the 400 GT name, with the maximum power output of just over 315 hp delivered at 6,500 rather than 7,000 rpm, the car now having a maximum speed of 260 kph (161.56 mph). The ZF gearbox and Salisbury differential combination was replaced with components assembled in Emilia. Porsche synchronizers were used in the gearbox, which was now more precise and quieter than the one previously fitted. Ferruccio Lamborghini's principal mission continued to be the creation of the "perfect" car, and he paid painstaking attention to every de-

tail. In this case, too, the contemporary press reviews were very positive, commenting on the 400 GT's smoothness and driveability even at high speeds. The car presented all the characteristics of a true Grand Tourer, definitively consecrating Lamborghini's place among the world's most significant marques, despite its youth compared with the automotive industry legends. Produced through 1968 in just over 280 examples, the 400 GT was chosen above all in the 2+2 configuration, with just twenty or so examples made in coupé form.

1966

MIURA

THE BIRTH OF AN ICON

LAMBORGHINI
1966

MIURA P400

Iconic. There is no better adjective to describe the Lamborghini Miura, a model that was capable not only of changing Lamborghini's own destiny but of also raising the bar within the supercar genre. It all began in 1965, when Lamborghini's stand at the Turin Motor Show featured a chassis with the engine and suspension from the 400 GT along with a host of innovative features. The first curiosity was that the chassis was exhibited at the behest of the engineers Giampaolo Dallara and Paolo Stanzani, who, despite Ferruccio Lamborghini's doubts, were convinced of the project's merits: an all-new chassis, with a structure in welded steel carrying all mechanical organs, with the V12 engine mounted transversally behind the driver.

The chassis caught the attention of the designer Nuccio Bertone, who recognized the potential of Dallara and Stanzani's creation. The styling of the bodywork was therefore entrusted to Carrozzeria Bertone and its young designer Marcello Gandini, who, in just four months, drew up lines destined for a place in automotive history. While the Miura legend had yet to explode, the choice of the name honored the Spanish breeder of fighting bulls, Don Eduardo Miura Fernandez, and the Lamborghini established enduring ties to the powerful animal. Following the rolling chassis exhibited in Turin, the Geneva Motor Show of 1966 saw the launch of the definitive Miura P400, with the car reveling in immediate worldwide success. Along with its unprecedented styling, the Miura was powered by a transverse 3.9 liter (238 cu. in.) V12 engine producing 350 cv (345.3 hp) at 7,000 rpm, good for a maximum speed of 300 kph (186.4 mph). Behind the birth of the first Lamborghini-badged supercar were numerous minor secrets, the result of production processes that had to pay careful attention to costs. For example, the Miura's legendary flip-up headlights were sourced from the Fiat 850 Spider, skillfully modified with the famous "eyelashes." Even though Ferruccio Lamborghini had initially seen the Miura as a marketing tool, with production limited to a few dozen examples, 108 examples were built in 1967 alone, sold at a list price of 7.7 million lire, and had an "official" delivery time of 270 days.

1966

WEBER
TIPO

Innovative styling, ample glazing, doors opening upward, and comfortable seats for four. The Lamborghini Marzal represents the forerunner of all the futuristic concept cars produced by the firm based in Sant'Agata Bolognese. Presented in 1967 at the Geneva Motor Show, the Marzal was designed by Marcello Gandini and was based on an elongated Miura chassis. It was fitted with a 1,965 cc (120 cu. in.) V6 engine producing 175 cv (172.6 hp) that was capable of propelling the car to a maximum speed of 225 kph (140 mph).

1967

MIURA P400 ROADSTER

While Ferruccio Lamborghini had invented the supercar concept with the Miura in 1966, with the Miura P400 Roadster, presented in 1968 at the Brussels Motor Show, he went even further, creating a one-off with perfect lines, destined to become the stuff of dreams for every collector.

Designed by Gandini and Bertone, the car changed significantly with the removal of the roof and side windows, but also with the significant modifications to the rear end, with the exposed 350 cv (345 hp) V12 engine, new lighting clusters, and a larger spoiler. With no provision for a roof but with the chassis reinforced to ensure that performance matched that of the closed version, the Miura P400 Roadster was never produced in series and was sold to the International Lead Zinc Research Organization (ILZRO), which replaced various components with others in zinc and lead, painted it in an iridescent golden green, and used it at length as a demonstration car. After multiple changes of ownership, the current proprietor thoroughly restored the P400 Roadster, returning it to its original 1968 state.

Right: The Miura P400 Roadster exhibited for the first time at the Brussels Motor Show. The car was open-topped and introduced a number of differences with respect to the closed version.

1968

FIAAM
FILTER
FAR-139

ISLERO

The Lamborghini Islero arrived after the Miura and represented a new model for a more traditionalist clientele. Based on the 400 GT, the Islero was styled by Mario Marazzi of the Carrozzeria firm following the closure of Touring. Under the hood was a 4-liter V12 producing 320 cv (315.7 hp) or 350 cv (345 hp) in Islero S form. The car was produced from 1968 to 1970, with 155 examples of the Islero and 70 of the Islero S built.

1968

ESPADA

From the outset of his adventure as a car manufacturer, Ferruccio Lamborghini was very clear about his aim to produce the finest GT on the roads, a fast, sporting car that would be both comfortable and luxuriously finished. The Espada 400 GT, presented at the Geneva Motor Show in March 1968 and designed by Paolo Stanzani and Marcello Gandini, was the car that for over a decade best represented this objective. The Espada in fact offered a cabin able to accommodate four adults comfortably, with more usable space for passengers and luggage than the earlier 2+2 400 GT and 2+2 Islero 400 GT models. The car was based around the 4-liter (239.8 cu. in.) 60° V12 engine, producing 325 cv (320 hp) at 7,200 rpm and 350 cv (345 hp) at 7,500 rpm in the Espada Series

II, presented in 1970. The world's fastest four-seater when it was presented, the Espada was produced in 1,226 examples divided into three series: 400 GT Series I from 1968 to 1969 in 176 examples, 400 GTE from 1970 to 1972 in 578 examples, and 400 GTS Series III from 1972 to 1978 in 472 examples.

1968

JARAMA 400 GT

THE LAST 2+2 GT

Named after an area north of Madrid famed for its fighting bull ranches, the Jarama represented the final evolution of the Lamborghini 2+2 GT coupé concept, powered by a front-mounted 4-liter (244 cu. in.) V12 engine. Developed on the basis of the earlier 400 GT and Islero models and retaining the same mechanical layout, the Jarama was distinguished by its Marcello Gandini styling for Carrozzeria Bertone, much more in line with the aesthetic canons of the 1970s, with taut, angular lines. The bodies of the pre-series examples were assembled by Carrozzeria Marazzi of Caronno Pertusella, which had just completed production of the Islero, while the production examples rolled off the Carrozzeria Bertone lines in the Grugliasco factory in the province of Turin. The year 1972 saw the debut of the Jarama GTS, which boasted a power output of 365 cv (360 hp) against the 350 cv (345 hp) of the first series. The uprated version was characterized by a transverse air intake on the hood and two air vents behind the front wheel arches. On sale from 1970 to 1976, 328 examples of the Jarama were produced.

1970

URRACO P250 GT

UP CLOSE

Born after what had been a turbulent period of industrial action, the Urraco made its debut at the 1970 Turin Motor Show and presented a brand-new feature for a Lamborghini badged car: a mid-mounted V8 engine displacing 2.5 liters (152.5 cu.in.) with a single overhead camshaft per bank. Just over 4.2 meters (13.78 feet) long, the "baby Lamborghini" was a 2+2 producing 220 cv (217 hp) at 7,800 rpm, which translated to a maximum speed of 245 kph (152 mph). Boasting innovative technical features for the era, thanks to the contribution of the engineer Paolo Stanzani, including the combination of a mid-mounted V8 engine and McPherson strut all-round independent suspension, the Urraco was designed by Marcello Gandini, then head of the styling department at Carrozzeria Bertone. Presented as the P250 Urraco, with the "P" standing for the rear or posterior location of the engine and "250" indicating the engine displacement (2.5 liters), the car was produced in 520 examples from 1970 to 1976. The Urraco was later shown at the 1974 Turin Motor Show in P200 form, with the displacement reduced to 1,994 cc (121.7 cu. in.) and a power output of 182 cv (179.5 hp), destined for the Italian market, where sixty-six examples were sold between 1975 and 1977. The successive P300 version (182.8 cu. in. for 261 hp) was presented in 1974 and produced from 1975 to 1979 in 190 examples.

1971

AN INSIDER'S STORY

Walter Rinaldi, Lamborghini's head of spare parts through 2009, tells his story: "I was a fifteen-year-old boy when I joined Lamborghini on the first of September 1966. The first time I saw the Miura? That would have been when it was loaded onto the transporter to be taken to the Turin Motor Show, where it was to be crowned queen of the event. The car's return from the Piedmont show marked the start of a magical period. It was barely a meter high; when you were sitting in it, you seemed to touch the asphalt. It had a spacious cabin, full of instruments and switches, and it was aggressive. It had the engine located transversally behind the cockpit, madness for that time; it was unique, as were its colors. The engineers Dallara and Stanzani, along with their team of technicians, created a fantastic car. It was then that production got underway, and I supplied the assembly line with hot and

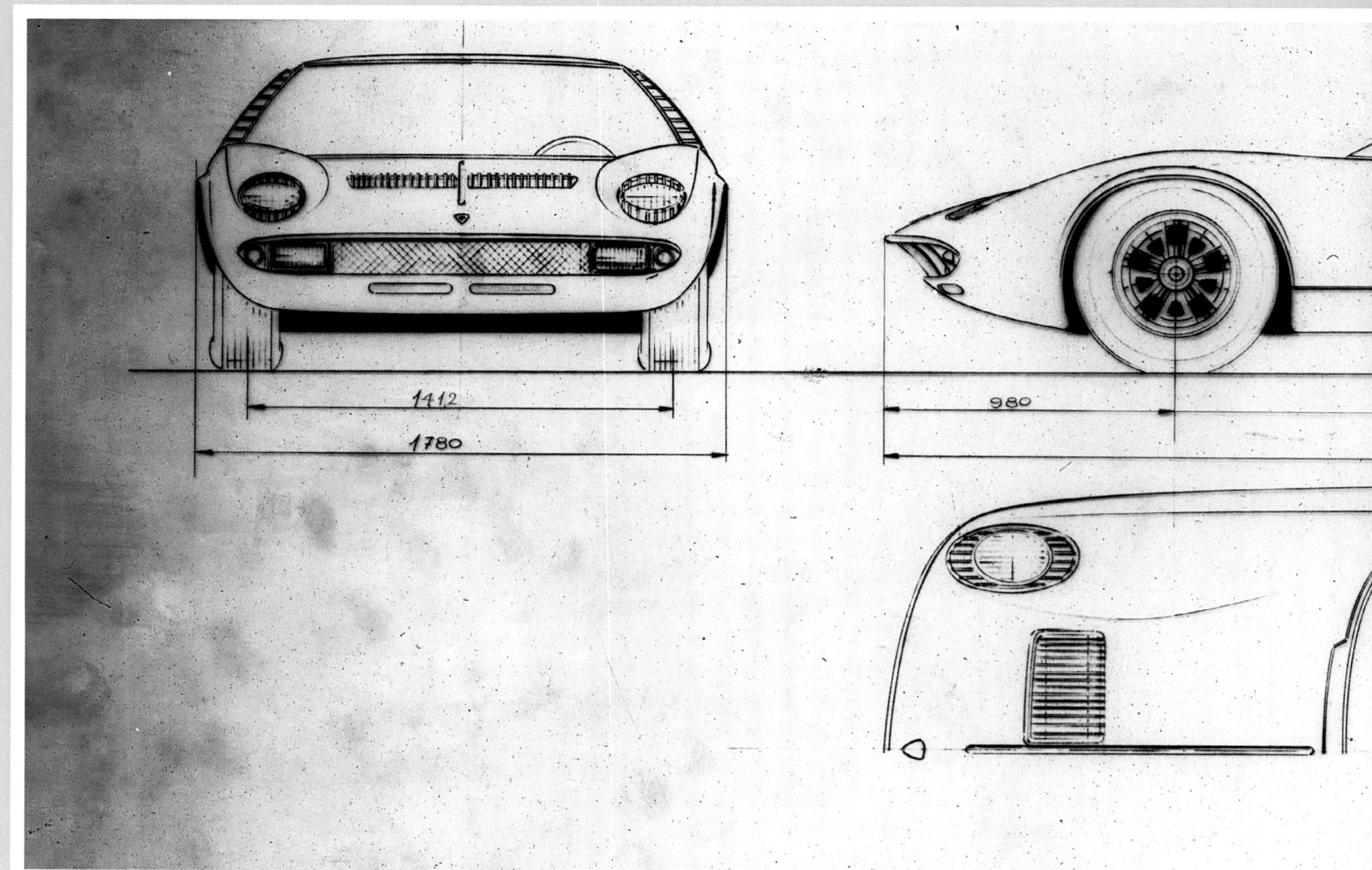

cold mechanical parts and also managed the parts store. Almost sixty years later, I still remember almost all the parts, their codes, and the suppliers of the era. Given my memory, I still help out at the Lamborghini Polo Storico, seeking out suppliers of mechanical parts and various commercial articles that are not easy to source. Actors, businessmen, and famous and stunningly beautiful women came to Lamborghini to buy the car and to see the colors and the interior trim, and I, young as I was, would be left speechless. Ferruccio Lamborghini would come to the factory; he would tour all the departments and always say hello to everyone, happy and proud to see his beautiful creature grow and be appreciated throughout the world. And so it was that this bolide of aluminum and steel changed automotive history."

Below: The official drawings of the Miura drafted by the Lamborghini Technical Department, with the dimensions of the car

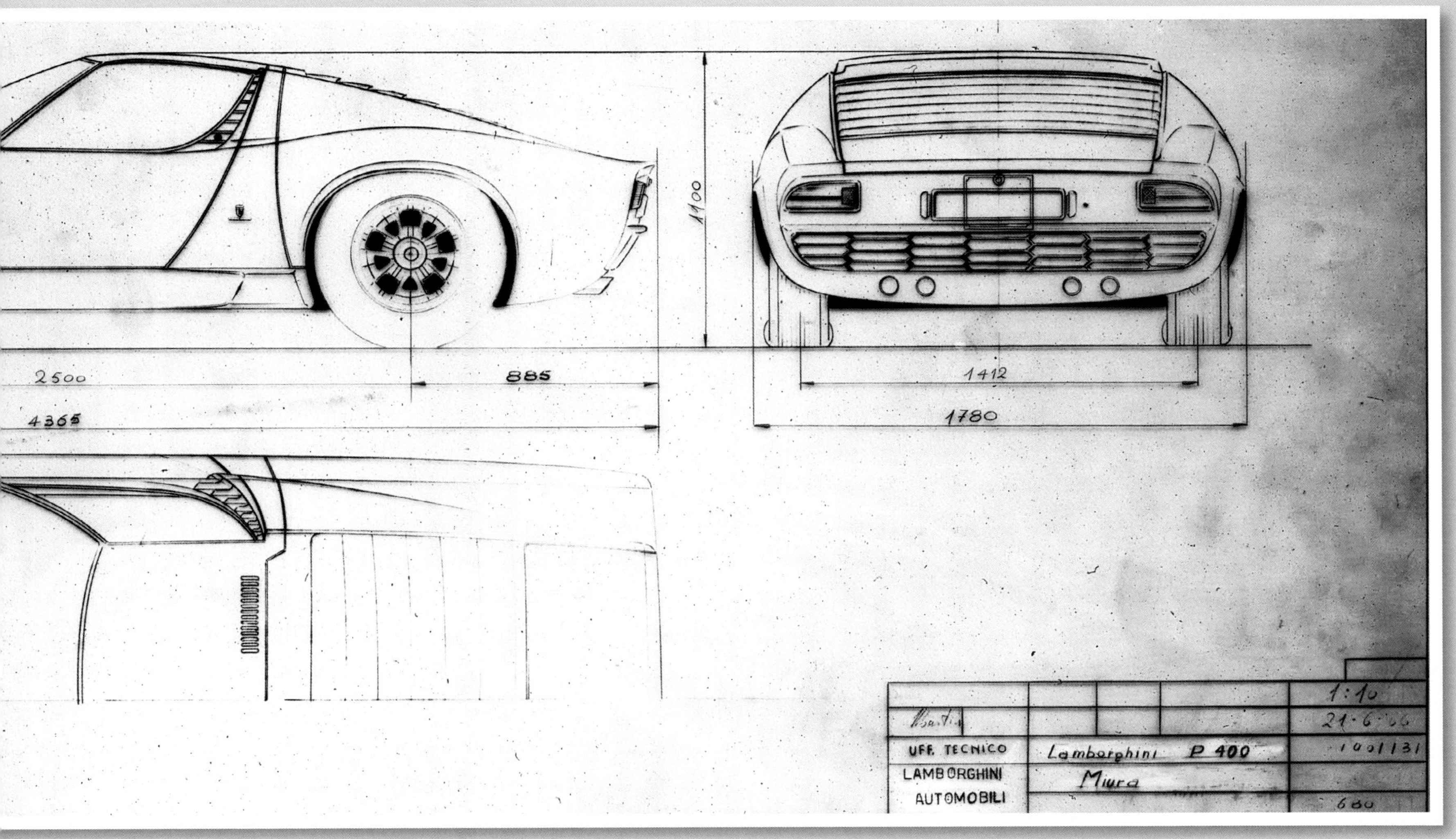

AT THE WHEEL OF THE MIURA SV

If you frame the QR code with the camera on your smartphone, you will be able to "climb aboard" the Lamborghini Miura SV thanks to exclusive footage created exclusively for this book. By turning up the volume, you will be able to listen to the symphony played by the V12, developing 385 cv (380 hp) and capable of propelling the car to a maximum speed of 300 kph (186 mph), reaching 100 kph (62 mph) from a standing start in just 5.7 seconds.

COUNTACH LP500

THE DEBUT

In March 1971 at the Geneva Motor Show, Automobili Lamborghini presented its "idea car," the LP500 Countach. The car immediately established itself as the queen of the show and was featured in all the leading automotive magazines throughout the world. This new model was conceived as a replacement for the legendary Miura and was to write a new chapter in motoring history, thanks both to its engineering and its styling. After a three-year development period, the LP500 was sacrificed in a crash test in March 1974 and then disappeared. It was to be reborn in 2021, fifty years later, after a labor of love lasting 25,000 hours led to its reconstruction by the Lamborghini Historical Department.

FROM FERRUCCIO'S FAREWELL TO THE ARRIVAL OF AUDI BY WAY OF THE DARK YEARS

1972/1998

AUTOMOBILI
LAMBORGHINI

NEW OWNERS AND ICONIC MODELS

Fewer than twenty years. Such was the period of time taken by Ferruccio Lamborghini to create a legendary marque capable of producing iconic models such as the Miura and Countach. The founder in fact sold 51 percent of his company in 1972 to a Swiss businessman, and in 1974 he ceded the remaining 49 percent, bidding farewell to the firm he had founded at Sant'Agata Bolognese in 1963.

While Ferruccio's departure was due to a number of factors—starting with the strikes in 1968, the sky-rocketing gas prices due to the Arab-Israeli war, the looming fuel crisis, and a lost order for more than 5,000 tractors due to the coup d'état in Bolivia—the following years were marked by that ongoing fuel crisis and the inexperience of the majority and minority shareholders Georges-Henri Rossetti and René Leimer. Despite the debut of the Countach, designed in the Ferruccio era but launched by the new owners, and the new V8 Urraco and Silhouette models, Lamborghini was forced into receivership.

1980 might have seen the return of Ferruccio Lamborghini to what was now his former company, but the Bologna Court rejected his proposal and instead chose the offer from Mimran, a French family, which in the summer of that year signed a commitment to save the company and the jobs it provided while investing the funds required to launch new models. Nuova Automobili Lamborghini was born in 1981 and over the following years was responsible for the production of models such as the Countach Quattrovalvole, the Jalpa, and the LM002. Led by the CEO, Emile Novaro, with the engineer Giulio Alfieri as technical director, the revived Lamborghini launched the redesigned V12 engine and introduced four valves per cylinder technology. The firm also introduced a marine engine that obtained excellent results in competition.

Everything changed in April 1987, when Mimran accepted an offer from Chrysler and sold the entire company. A simple meeting between Novaro and the Detroit company regarding the supply of an eight-cylinder engine to be fitted to the heir of the Jalpa led to the change in ownership, thanks to the intuition of the chairman and CEO of the American marque, Lee Iacocca. After years of uncertainty, the Lamborghini employees could finally count on the economic and industrial stability offered by a major manufacturer such as Chrysler. The year 1990 saw the debut of the Diablo, the most important model launched under the American ownership, with all-wheel drive later being introduced on a Sant'Agata Bolognese supercar for the first time. However, as had happened in the past, everything changed rapidly when Chrysler sold the company to Megatech, a Bermuda-registered holding company with 60 percent Indonesian and 40 percent Malaysian capital. In reality, Lamborghini had passed into the hands of Hutomo "Tommy" Mandala Putra Suharto, who received it as a gift from the fabulously wealthy Indonesian president and dictator. The darkest period in Lamborghini's history was approaching.

Production output fell to an all-time low in 1995, with only just over 200 cars being produced by a company employing around 200 people. That same year, the Diablo Roadster made its debut, an open-top version of the coupé, then the only model in the Lamborghini range. Led by Vittorio di Capua, Lamborghini was navigating increasingly troubled waters. However, in the best local traditions, Emilian stubbornness led to radical changes. In 1997, there was a meeting between Lamborghini and Audi; the objective was the supply of the eight-cylinder engine fitted to the Audi A8 flagship for use in the future "Baby Diablo," which was to lead to the birth of the Gallardo. The idea, which had come to Maurizio Reggiani, Lamborghini's future chief technical officer, was to locate the V8 at the rear, swinging it through 180 degrees. Negotiations proceeded for around eight months, through January 1998 and the Detroit Motor Show, where the Audi chiefs informed Reggiani of their decision to supply the engine, but on one condition: that Audi would buy Lamborghini. Despite the excellent offer, the operation risked collapsing due to the demands of the Indonesian shareholder, who was determined to retain an interest in the company rather than sell it outright. This was an outcome the Ingolstadt marque refused to take into consideration, insisting on full ownership of the company. In this case, too, "providence" came to the aid of the deal, thanks to a coup d'état in Indonesia that forced Tommy Suharto to give in. The Lamborghini renaissance could finally get underway.

COUNTACH LP400

1974

UP CLOSE

Ferruccio Lamborghini had done it again: He had created a car capable of setting new standards and rendering all its rivals obsolete. Having done it with the Miura, he did it again with the Lamborghini Countach. The last car produced under the control of Ferruccio, who left the company after selling 51 percent of his share to Georges-Henri Rossetti in 1972 and the remaining 49 percent to René Leimer in 1974, the Countach LP400 perfectly encapsulated the Lamborghini DNA, composed of innovation, a search for the extreme, and above all, a capacity to arouse wonder and emotion. The very name "Countach" came from a Piedmontese exclamation of wonder pronounced by one of Marcello Gandini's team when he saw the car for the first time. Little more than a meter (3.3 feet) high and weighing just 1,065 kilos (2,205 lbs.), the LP was built around a tubular steel chassis and powered by a V12 engine displacing 3,929 cc (just under 240 cu. in.) and producing 370 hp, mounted longitudinally and capable of providing a maximum speed of 192 mph. Gandini also introduced the upward-opening doors that have become something of a trademark of the cars produced at Sant'Agata Bolognese. Characterized by fenders without flares and a roof with a central indent dedicated to the rearview mirror that earned it the "periscope" nickname, the LP400 was produced between 1974 and 1978 in 151 examples.

THE COUNTACH PRODUCTION LINE

It was March 1974 when series production of the Countach began in the Lamborghini factory at Sant'Agata Bolognese. The model was to become an automotive legend and remain in production for no less than sixteen years. The Countach was the first Lamborghini for which the body was constructed and hand-beaten in-house. Up until then, in fact, all the Lamborghinis had originated at two different sites, with the mechanical parts being fabricated by Lamborghini itself and the bodies by outside coachbuilders who would then send them to Sant'Agata Bolognese to be fitted to the rolling chassis. The decision to produce the bodies of the new car within the Lamborghini factory had an immediate and significant effect on the growth of the

company. During the Countach years, the assembly line was simple and craft-based, with everything being done by hand. The bodywork panels were beaten and checked on a wooden jig before being welded to one another and adjusted on the so-called "cala" or "dolly." This last phase was fundamental, given that every part, having been produced and assembled by hand, was only apparently identical to the next on the line but in reality was actually different. The complete bodyshell, still in unpainted aluminum, was then mated to the chassis. Mounted on an industrial carriage running on tracks, the assembly was then moved from one station to the next, where the various mechanical components were fitted. The Countach also inaugurated Lamborghini's in-house upholstery department.

1974

SILHOUETTE

The first all-new model created after Ferruccio Lamborghini's departure, the Silhouette, which represented an evolution of the Urraco, proposed a targa-topped alternative designed to conquer the complex American market. In the meantime, the V8 engine had been developed and in its 3-liter (183 cu. in.) version was fitted with four overhead camshafts and provided a maximum speed of 260 kph (161.5 mph). Despite having excellent commercial potential on paper, following the two prototypes, Lamborgini produced just fifty-three examples of the Silhouette, the last of them being used and tested as a prototype for the Jalpa.

silhouette
1976

CHEETAH

A Lamborghini for use in war zones? It might have been possible had the Sant'Agata Bolognese company won the American military order. However, that order went elsewhere, and the Cheetah, powered by a Chrysler V8 engine developing 180 cv (177 hp), remained a one-off example of Lamborghini creativity. Nonetheless, the project was by no means wasted. We simply had to wait a few years to see the birth of the LM001 and LM002, the second being the world's first true super SUV thanks to the adoption of the V12 engine from the Lamborghini Countach.

1977

COUNTACH 400 S

The Lamborghini Countach LP 400 S was used in the film *Cannonball Run*. Produced in November 1979, it was finished in black with mustard upholstery. It was modified for the film with a wing and two spotlights at the front, a spoiler, three aerials, and twelve exhaust pipes.

The Lamborghini Countach LP 400, produced from 1978 to 1982 in 235 examples, was derived directly from the LP 400 special, which the Canadian enthusiast Walter Wolf had built to order by Lamborghini. The LP 400 S was characterized by the adoption of low-profile Pirelli tires, flared wheel arches, magnesium wheels with a "telephone dial" design, an aerodynamic appendage below the nose, and, on request, a rear wing, before it became one of the distinguishing features of the Countach in later years. The model was again powered by the 3,929 cc (240 cu. in.) V12 producing 353 cv (348 hp) at 7,500 rpm and was capable of reaching 285 mph (177 mph). Lamborghini produced the 5000 S between 1982 and 1984 in 323 examples, with only minor styling differences. The V12 engine was enlarged to 4.8 liters (293 cu. in.) and produced 375 cv (370 hp), which was good for a maximum speed of 300 kph (186.4 mph).

1978

JALPA

The 1981 Geneva Motor Show: The Jalpa makes its debut on the Lamborghini stand, born under the ownership of the Mimran family. The bodywork, with the targa-type opening roof, was the work of Marc Deschamps, head of the styling department at Carrozzeria Bertone, with the influence and contribution of engineer Giulio Alfieri, at that time the general and technical director at Lamborghini. The most significant technical innovation came with the increase in the displacement of the aluminum 90° V8 engine to 3.5 liters (213.5 cu. in.). The unit now produced a maximum power output of 255 cv (251.56 hp). The model went into production in 1982, with the second series being presented at the 1984 Geneva Motor Show. It was eventually dropped in 1988, after 420 cars had been produced.

1981

COUNTACH QUATTROVALVOLE

The years passed, but the Lamborghini Countach continued to be the supercar to beat. Over a decade after the model's launch, the Countach Quattrovalvole represented a major update, with the V12 engine's displacement increased to just over 315 cu. in. The name, derived from the new four valves per cylinder configuration—hence the Quattrovalvole or QV designation—saw the overall power output reach 449 hp. The styling modifications were instead more limited, with the introduction of an extra 1.7 inches to the front track and a new engine cover designed to house the Weber carburetors mounted vertically rather than horizontally. In the best Countach traditions, the performance figures represented benchmarks, with the V12 built at Sant'Agata Bolognese capable of propelling the car from a standing start to 62 mph in just five seconds, topping out at a maximum of 186.4 mph. All this, as was always the case at that time, was without any driving aids.

1985

PIRELLI
SCORPION
ZERO

LAMBORGHINI LM002

THE WORLD'S FIRST SUPER SUV

The model destined for production as the Lamborghini LM002 was presented for the first time at the Brussels Motor Show in 1986 and went on to define the final design; the V12 derived from the Countach Quattrovalvole engine had a displacement of just over 315 cu. in and produced 444 hp at 6,800 rpm. With bodywork in aluminum and fiberglass, the car boasted four-wheel drive, a two-speed transfer box, and a self-locking central differential. It was capable of tackling slopes of 120 percent. Reaching a maximum speed of over 124 mph, the LM002 was fitted with specially designed Pirelli Scorpion tires that allowed it to tackle loose surfaces, such as sand, while continuing to offer excellent durability in hot climates. Production of the bodyshells began at a company in Bilbao, Spain. The partly finished assemblies were then sent to Sant'Agata Bolognese to be completed with the engine, mechanical components, and trim and be tested and delivered. The final touch was the luxurious interior, created on the basis of the specific demands of the client. Between 1986 and 1992, a total of 300 units were manufactured. This was the world's first true super SUV, since anothing like the 444 hp V12 off-roader had ever been seen before. The LM002 anticipated the fashion for high-performance SUVs by thirty years.

1986

COUNTACH 25TH ANNIVERSARIO

Between 1988 and 1990, Lamborghini produced 658 examples of the Countach 25th Anniversario, a special model created to celebrate the manufacturer's first twenty-five years and present a thorough revision of the Countach's aerodynamic appendages. The air intakes on the rear fenders and several panels such as the front and rear hoods were made in carbon fiber for the first time. It should be noted that the Countach's commercial success followed a constantly upward trajectory, and the last two versions were produced in the greatest numbers, benefiting from the model's homologation for sale on the American market.

1988

AT THE WHEEL OF THE COUNTACH 25TH ANNIVERSARIO

If you frame the QR code with the camera on your smartphone, you will be able to "climb aboard" the Lamborghini Countach 25th Anniversario. By turning up the volume, you will be able to listen to the sound of the 5,167 cc (315 cu. in.) V12 delivering 385 cv (449 hp) to the rear wheels at 7,000 rpm. Capable of a maximum speed of 295 kph (183 mph), the Countach 25th Anniversario presented cleaner lines and a luxurious interior complete with accessories such as air conditioning.

On the road, the Lamborghini Countach 25th Anniversario shows all its character, starting from the steering, which was precise for the time but by no means light. While a modern Lamborghini is a "domesticated" supercar, the Countach requires the utmost concentration at all times. Everything has to handle firmly, starting with the gear change, with first gear to the rear left and used according to the selector gate. Changes are slick and precise, while the small pedals should be used decisively but without unnecessary jerking. The sound of the Countach V12 is something every car enthusiast should listen to at least once in their lifetime, giving thanks to the work done at Sant'Agata Bolognese forty years ago.

THE BIRTH OF THE DIABLO

There was a five-year wait to see the heir to the Countach. It was 1985 when Lamborghini set to work on Project 132, with the objective of bringing to life the next in a successful series of V12 supercars. The Diablo was unveiled in 1990, the fruit of a design by Marcello Gandini, later partially revised by the Styling Center at Chrysler, the American manufacturer having become the majority shareholder in the company founded by Ferruccio Lamborghini. The car had a classic mechanical layout with a 5.7-liter (348 cu. in.), twelve-cylinder engine fitted with direct fuel injection and producing 492 cv (485 hp) delivered to the rear wheels and guaranteeing a maximum speed of 325 kph (202 mph). All this was combined with a leather-upholstered interior, with air conditioning and electrically adjustable seats. The Diablo nonetheless remained a purist's supercar, with no driving aids, not even power steering. For that we had to wait until 1993.

1990

DIABLO VT AND SE

Three years after its debut, the Diablo became the first Lamborghini coupé to be equipped with all-wheel drive, something that over the years has become a distinguishing feature of the supercars produced at Sant'Agata Bolognese. Developed by engineers Luigi Marmiroli and Maurizio Reggiani—with support from the World Rally Champion Sandro Munari, who worked with Lamborghini for a couple of years—the Diablo VT (Viscous Traction) introduced a viscous coupling capable of splitting the torque at the front differential, thereby rendering the car more manageable. Electronically controlled suspension with five different settings was also introduced. The SE special edition also debuted in 1993, marking the thirtieth anniversary of the founding of the car manufacturing by Ferruccio Lamborghini, a model recognizable thanks to its exclusively purple livery and a power output of 425 cv (518 hp). In terms of numbers, the Diablo VT was produced in 529 examples from 1993 to 1998, and the SE in 157 from 1993 to 1994.

1993

Motorcraft KDV-2
Lamborghini

FIRING ORDER
1-7-4-10-2-8-6-12-3-9-5-11
CAUTION !
HIGH TEMPERATURE

DIABLO VT ROADSTER

The first open-top Lamborghini: this was the proud boast of the Lamborghini Diablo Roadster, presented as a prototype at the Geneva Motor Show in 1992 and in definitive form at the Paris Show in 1995. Created around the rolling chassis of the VT, the V12 engine delivered 492 cv (485 hp) to the four driving wheels, providing for a maximum speed of 323 kph (just over 200 mph) and a 0-to-100 kph (0-to-62 mph) sprint in as little as 4.1 seconds. The carbon fiber roof panel could be stowed above the engine cover.

1995

P Zero

In 1996 the world of racing earned a definitive place in the Lamborghini story. Following the Miura Jota, a one-off conceived for racing in 1970, the Sant'Agata Bolognese manufacturer finally committed to taking to the track with a racing program. To do so, it created the Diablo SV, a road-going model with a racing character, starting with its reduced weight, exclusively rear-wheel drive, and extreme aerodynamics. This car formed the basis for the Diablo SV-R, created to participate in the newly organized Supertrophy single marque series.

1996

FROM THE ACQUISITION BY AUDI TO THE BIRTH OF THE THIRD MODEL

1998/2015

AUTOMOBILI
LAMBORGHINI

THE GROWTH OF AUTOMOBILI LAMBORGHINI

Less than five years had passed since Lamborghini's darkest times, but by 1998, there was a new feeling around Sant'Agata Bolognese. Thanks to its acquisition by Audi, the company founded in 1963 by Ferruccio Lamborghini could count for the first time on stable ownership with a real long-term vision. Just four years sufficed for the complete renewal of the range, with the Murciélago replacing the Diablo in 2001 and the debut in 2003 of the Gallardo, powered by the new naturally aspirated V10 engine. Production volumes also changed; while it had taken over ten years, from 1990 to 2001, for just over 2,900 examples of the Diablo to be produced, the Gallardo reached 3,000 units in just over two years. Thanks to a greater focus on quality and a range of thirty-five different versions, this figure would exceed 14,000 examples by the end of the model's production run, ten years after its debut. From its first appearance in 2003, the Gallardo represented a watershed in the history of Automobili Lamborghini: In its first forty years, the company had produced an average of about 250 supercars per year. Instead, during the decade of the Gallardo, production soared to very different levels, with volumes stabilizing at around 2,000 units per year. The Centro Stile Lamborghini was established in 2001, directed, in chronological order, by Luc Donckerwolke, Filippo Perini, and Walter de Silva, before the arrival of Mitja Borkert.

In 2005, Stephan Winkelmann was appointed CEO, and Lamborghini took another leap forward in terms of quality and future growth. Further innovations came out of major investments in the development and application of lightweight carbon fiber materials. While the first composite materials department was established in 1983, thanks to the expertise developed with the carbon fiber and Kevlar components for the Boeing 767, and the Countach Evoluzione was launched (the first Lamborghini model to use composite materials), 2007 instead saw the company begin collaborating with the University of Washington. This marked an important turning point for the development of out-of-autoclave RTM (resin transfer molding) technology, which was then to be the basis for the monocoque of the future Aventador. In 2008 the first working partnership agreement was signed with Boeing, thanks to which Lamborghini began to study the crash behavior of composite materials and implement technologies, processes, and methods of simulation and characterization typical of the aeronautics and aerospace industries. In 2010, the Forged Composites® technology was launched, the specific patent for which led to the idea for the Sesto Elemento supercar. That same year, the Lamborghini factory opened a plant dedicated to the production of components in composite materials, which alternates phases of automated processing with phases of painstaking craftsmanship.

In 2011, the Aventador was launched, the first Lamborghini model made entirely of carbon fiber. The innovative monocoque, produced using the "RTM-Lambo" technology, guarantees a chassis weighing only 229.5 kilos (506 lbs.) and paved the way for a future with a wealth of experimentation. In 2014, the Lamborghini repair service for carbon fiber cars obtained TÜV (Technischer Überwachungsverein) certification, while 2015 saw the introduction of Carbonskin®, an innovative material protected by an exclusive Lamborghini patent. Going back a few years, the Urus Concept was unveiled in 2012, while in 2013 the Egoista single-seater show car was presented to celebrate the marque's fiftieth anniversary.

In addition, a new photovoltaic system was installed at the Sant'Agata Bolognese plant and inaugurated in February 2013. This was the largest integrated system in the industrial sector in Emilia-Romagna and, together with other measures, enabled a 30 percent reduction in carbon dioxide emissions, the equivalent of more than 1,067 tons per year. The operation involves major industrial areas such as the production plant, the commercial offices, the after-sales department, and the Centro Stile, for a total of 17,000 square meters (183,000 sq. ft.), an area greater than two football fields.

The year 2014 was the Huracán's debut, and in 2015, for the first time in Lamborghini's history, the company delivered more than 3,000 cars. With a sales network of 135 dealers in fifty countries, deliveries to customers grew from 2,530 units to 3,245 in 2015, a result translating to an increase of 28 percent over the previous year, two and a half times the sales volume of 2010. Lamborghini's new era had officially begun, with work starting on the production of the third model: the Urus.

1998

DIABLO GTR

The first Lamborghinis produced under the aegis of Audi: the Diablo GT and GTR, the latter produced in just thirty examples destined for competition use. Powered by the V12 engine, with the displacement increased from 5,707 cc (348.26 cu. in.) to 5,992 cc (365.65 cu. in.), the power output also rose by 55 cv (around 52 hp) to a total of 575 cv (around 567 hp).

1999

Lamborghini

6.0 L
V12
GTR
GTR

AT THE WHEEL OF THE DIABLO 6.0

In 2000 the Lamborghini Diablo 6.0 raised the bar, with its styling, interior, and performance all improved. The 6-liter (366 cu. in.) V12 engine delivered 550 cv (542.58 hp) to the four driven wheels, which was good for acceleration from 0 to 100 kph (0 to 62 mph) in less than four seconds. The car featured in our present-day test is the 2001 Diablo SE 6.0 L finished in Elios Gold, one of the forty-four examples produced. Compared with the Countach, everything was now more convenient and painstakingly finished, with a much-improved driving position. Climbing aboard after having literally raised the door, you are welcomed by the hip-hugging sports seats upholstered in tan hide and a cockpit characterized by fine leathers and carbon fiber. The dashboard, finished in leather and carbon fiber, boasts seven round analog instruments with the rev counter to the fore; the central console is small and contains only the stereo system, the heating and air conditioning controls, and the leather-trimmed ashtray, an accessory unthinkable on today's cars. The steering and gear change are lighter, as is the braking system, which now features ABS. Beware though; the Diablo always needs to be treated with respect, since the V12 boasts almost infinite power, and the car can become truly demanding on the limit, especially in low-grip situations. This model was fitted with the VT all-wheel-drive system as standard, lending the Lamborghini substantially neutral and secure handling, even through demanding corners at high speeds. The steering is precise, heavy, and progressive to the right point, the Lambo unhesitatingly following the lines, while the disc brakes, equipped with ABS, are powerful and fade-free, despite a weight in running order of more than 1,000 kilos (2,205 lbs.). The wheels have 18-inch rims and are fitted with 235/35 ZR and 335/30 ZR rubber at the front and rear, respectively. Rear visibility is virtually nonexistent, but the two large side mirrors help when overtaking. The situation is different when you have to park in reverse; in this case, we use the technique developed by the historic Lamborghini tester Balboni: door open, sitting on the sill, legs stretching to reach the pedals. An operation almost as tricky as taking a Diablo to the limit.

By framing the QR code with the camera on your smartphone, you will be able to "climb aboard" the Lamborghini Diablo 6.0 thanks to a camera car created exclusively for this book. By turning up the volume, you will be able to listen to the howl of the 6-liter, 12-cylinder engine producing 550 cv (542.5 hp) and experience the emotions of a legendary supercar.

THE BIRTH OF MOTORSPORT

Motorsport has always been a part of the Lamborghini DNA. Despite Ferruccio Lamborghini's decision not to make the Raging Bull racing an official works team, from the time of the Miura Jota, the competition world was integral to the cars produced at Sant'Agata Bolognese. Following the experience in Formula 1 with the production of the LE3512 engine in 1989 and with the Lambo 291 single-seater in 1991, the birth of Motorsport Lamborghini coincided with the creation of the Diablo GTR. Produced in 1999 in just thirty examples destined for competition use, this model was the forerunner of a tradition in the world of racing that has become one of the pillars of the Emilian firm's success. The Diablo GTR was actually the only Lamborghini V12 used in covered wheel racing, the architecture being superseded by the V10 units powering the Gallardo and Huracán.

BLANCPAIN
BLANCPAIN
IMPERIALE
SUPER TROFEO
LEAD CAR

THE BIRTH OF THE MURCIÉLAGO

Right: The LP 640 Versace, produced in a limited edition in 2006 and finished in either white or black

Below: The LP 580 was characterized by a height of just 120 cm (47.24 inches) and the scissor doors.

The 2001 Frankfurt Motor Show: The new millennium had only just gotten underway, and Lamborghini was revealing its new V12; the Murciélago picked up where true automotive icons such as the Miura, Countach, and Diablo had left off. The first brand-new model created under the Audi ownership, the Murciélago combined the best of the German and Italian automotive industries, with significantly improved build quality and the performance of a true Sant'Agata Bolognese supercar. As ever, the name came from the bullfighting world. Murciélago, which in Spanish means "bat," was a bull that during a corrida in the Córdoba arena in 1879 survived no fewer than twenty-four lances. Spared due to its courage, it was presented to Don Antonio Miura and sired the line of Miura bulls.

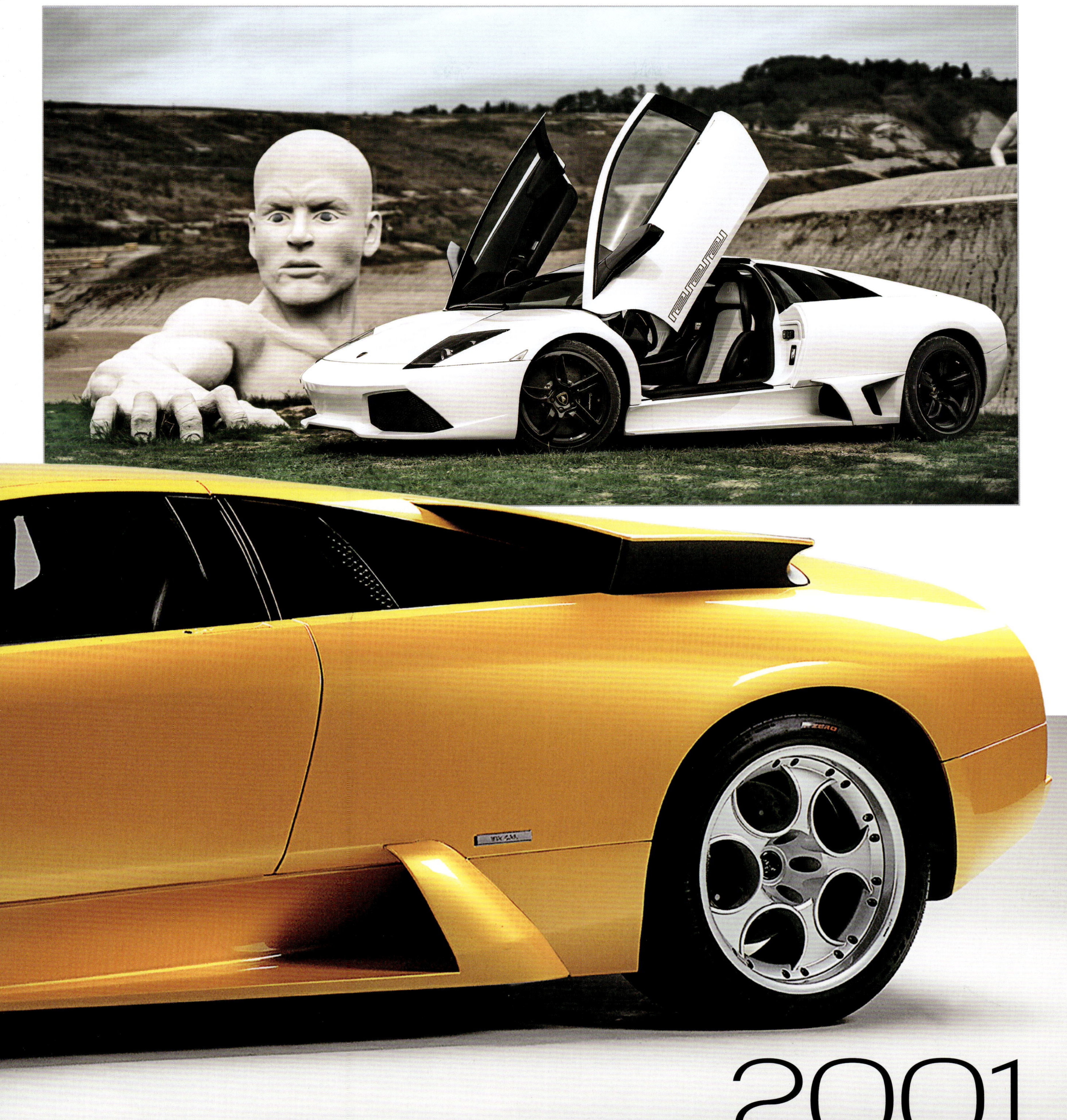

2001

UP CLOSE

The styling was the work of Lamborghini's Centro Stile, then directed by Luc Donckerwolke. It featured clean lines and new features such as a cooling system that automatically opened and closed according to the conditions of use. All the Murciélago variants were fitted with all-wheel drive, the system inherited from the Diablo featuring a Ferguson viscous coupling capable of splitting the torque through to a maximum of 70 percent going to the rear wheels and 30 percent to the front. The chassis was in carbon fiber with a composite floorpan structure in aluminum and at the launch of the car, was the stiffest load-bearing structure ever produced by Lamborghini. The running gear was completely revised with a new suspension and new geometries.

Mechanically, the differences with respect to the Diablo 6.0 VT were less accentuated, with the same longitudinal mid-mounted V12 engine. The displacement and power output were instead different, with 6.2 liters (378.34 cu. in.) now producing 580 cv (around 572 hp) at 7,200 rpm. The gearbox was fitted with six speeds and mated to a significantly lighter clutch than the Diablo. Maximum speed? 330 kph (205 mph), with acceleration from 0 to 100 kph (0 to 62 mph) in 3.8 seconds.

THE BIRTH OF THE GALLARDO

The Geneva Motor Show 2003: Automobili Lamborghini presents the Gallardo. The full potential of the "Baby Lambo" was immediately apparent thanks to the fresh styling and the 367.75 hp, V10 engine fitted to a Lamborghini for the first time. The design work began in 2000, on the basis of an initial proposal by Italdesign Giugiaro, subsequently optimized and completed by the recently formed Centro Stile Lamborghini led by Donckerwolke. It was with the Gallardo that in May 2004 the company began the tradition of donating cars to the Italian police, the vehicles being used for special services, such as carrying transplant organs and lifesaving drugs, or ceremonial duties.

2003

MURCIÉLAGO ROADSTER

A top speed of around 340 kph (211 mph) with an open top: The Murciélago Roadster added a new open-top V12 to the Lamborghini story, combining the styling of the coupé with a series of new features designed to enhance its safety and appeal. There were new air intakes and head restraints with roll bars that would automatically deploy should the car overturn. Boasting a stiffer chassis, the Murciélago Roadster added a subframe above the V12 engine. Two gearboxes were available: the manual six-speed and the automatic electro-hydraulic "eGear" system.

2004

The essence of the marque. A design icon produced in just twenty examples. Such was the description of the Lamborghini Reventón, presented at the 2007 Frankfurt Motor Show. Sold at the time for a million euros in coupé form, the car boasted innovative styling by new chief designer Filippo Perini, although it was based on the Murciélago LP640. The front section was characterized by the acute angle of the arrowhead in the center and by the muscular, forward-facing air intakes.

The name "Reventón" was chosen in line with the long tradition of bullfighting references. Reventón in fact refers to the name of a fighting bull belonging to the family of Don Rodriguez, known above all for having killed the matador Felix Guzman in 1943. The Roadster version was presented in 2009 and produced in fifteen examples.

REVENTÓN

2007

GALLARDO LP 560-4 SPYDER

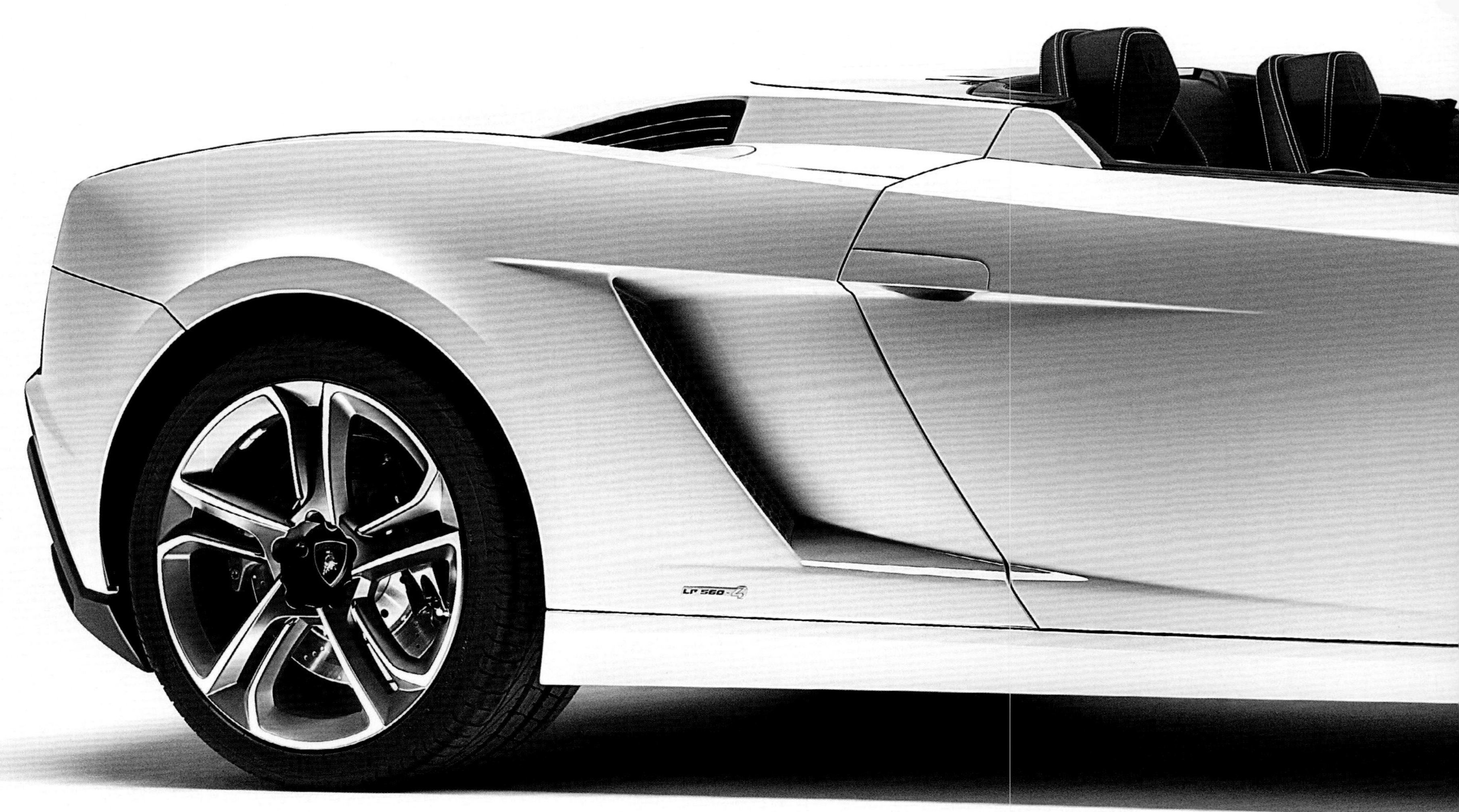

The first open-top V10 produced by Lamborghini, the Gallardo LP 560-4 Spyder debuted in 2008 and represented a road-going model of immense appeal. Below the rear engine cover was the 10-cylinder power unit, displacing around 5,204 cc (317.5 cu. in.), combined with the permanent all-wheel-drive system and a declared power output of 570 cv (419.2 hp). Thanks to its low weight, the LP 560-4 Spyder was capable of a maximum speed of around 325 kph (202 mph) and a 0 to 100 kph (0 to 62 mph) sprint in 3.4 seconds. All this was combined with the thrill of driving with the wind in your hair.

2008

MURCIÉLAGO LP 650-4 ROADSTER

2009

No roof and 660 cv (652 hp). In 2009 the Lamborghini Murciélago LP 650-4 Roadster, produced in just fifty examples, became the most powerful open-top Lamborghini in the history of Sant'Agata Bolognese and was capable of a remarkable 330 kph (205 mph). The figures were slightly better for the coupé, with the 6.5-liter (396.65 cu. in.) V12 producing around 661 hp (670 cv; hence the 670-4 SV designation), the weight dropped to 1,560 kilos (2,205 lbs.), and the maximum speed rose to around 340 kph (211 mph). Both versions were equipped with all-wheel drive and six-speed eGear transmission.

By framing the QR code with the camera on your smartphone, you will be able to "climb aboard" the Lamborghini Murciélago LP 650-4 Roadster thanks to a camera car created exclusively for this book.

BLANCPAIN
BLANCPAIN
BLANCPAIN
BLANCPAIN
PPG
PETRICORSE
IMPERIALE
PIRELLI
22
22
24
REITER EN

THE BIRTH OF THE SUPER TROFEO

In 2009, four years before the creation of Squadra Corse, the Lamborghini Super Trofeo was introduced in Europe. The protagonist of the single-marque series was the Lamborghini Gallardo, powered by the V10 engine developing 560 cv (552.5 hp). The added value of the car from Sant'Agata Bolognese was provided by the all-wheel-drive system perfected by the Squadra Corse engineers to guarantee exceptional traction out of corners and great stability even in low-grip conditions. Added to this was a perfect balance among performance, reliability, and running costs, a combination capable of ensuring great success from the earliest years of the single-marque championship. The championship expanded, arriving in Asia in 2012 and North America the following year. Given the great success of the Super Trofeo, the logical next step was to develop a similar project for racing in the GT3 category.

2009

SESTO ELEMENTO

2010

Less than 1,000 kilos (2,204 lbs.) in weight and with a power output of 570 cv (562.2 hp): The Lamborghini Sesto Elemento debuted at the Paris Motor Show in 2010, displaying the Emilian firm's capacity for working with carbon fiber. Accredited with an extraordinary weight-to-power ratio of just 1.75 kg/cv (around 3.9 lbs./hp) and the ability to sprint from 0 to 100 kph (0 to 62 mph) in just two to five seconds, the Sesto Elemento took its name from the periodic table, in which carbon is the sixth element. Produced in just twenty examples, this model provided evidence of Lamborghini's world-leading carbon fiber reinforced plastic (CFRP) technology capabilities. The Emilian marque developed this technology in its two research centers, the ACRC (Advanced Composites Research Center) at Sant'Agata Bolognese and the ACSL (Advanced Composite Structure Laboratory) in Seattle, where it cooperates with the University of Washington and the Boeing aerospace company. The styling was also innovative, with the front and rear sections of the bodywork being single pieces. The Lamborghini engineers coined the term "cofango," a portmanteau word combining "cofano" (hood) and "parafango" (fender). These large components were secured with easily removable screws to permit rapid disassembly. The cofango also referenced an icon from the marque's past: In 1966 the legendary Lamborghini Miura was the only supercar with a mid-mounted engine and one-piece opening rear bodywork.

GALLARDO LP 570-4 SUPERLEGGERA

Compared to the Gallardo LP 560-4, the total weight of the Gallardo LP 570-4 Superleggera was reduced by around 70 kilos (154 lbs.) through widespread use of carbon fiber. The Sant'Agata Bolognese supercar tipped the scales at a dry weight of 1,340 kg (2,954.19 lbs.), while the 5.2-liter (317.3 cu. in.) V10 engine now produced a maximum power output of 560 cv (562.3 hp), resulting in a weight-to-power ratio of 2.35 kg/cv (5.35 lbs./hp). On the road, the Superleggera had a declared maximum speed of 325 kph (201.95 mph) and a 0 to 100 kph (0 to 62 mph) time of just 3.4 seconds.

2010

AVENTADOR

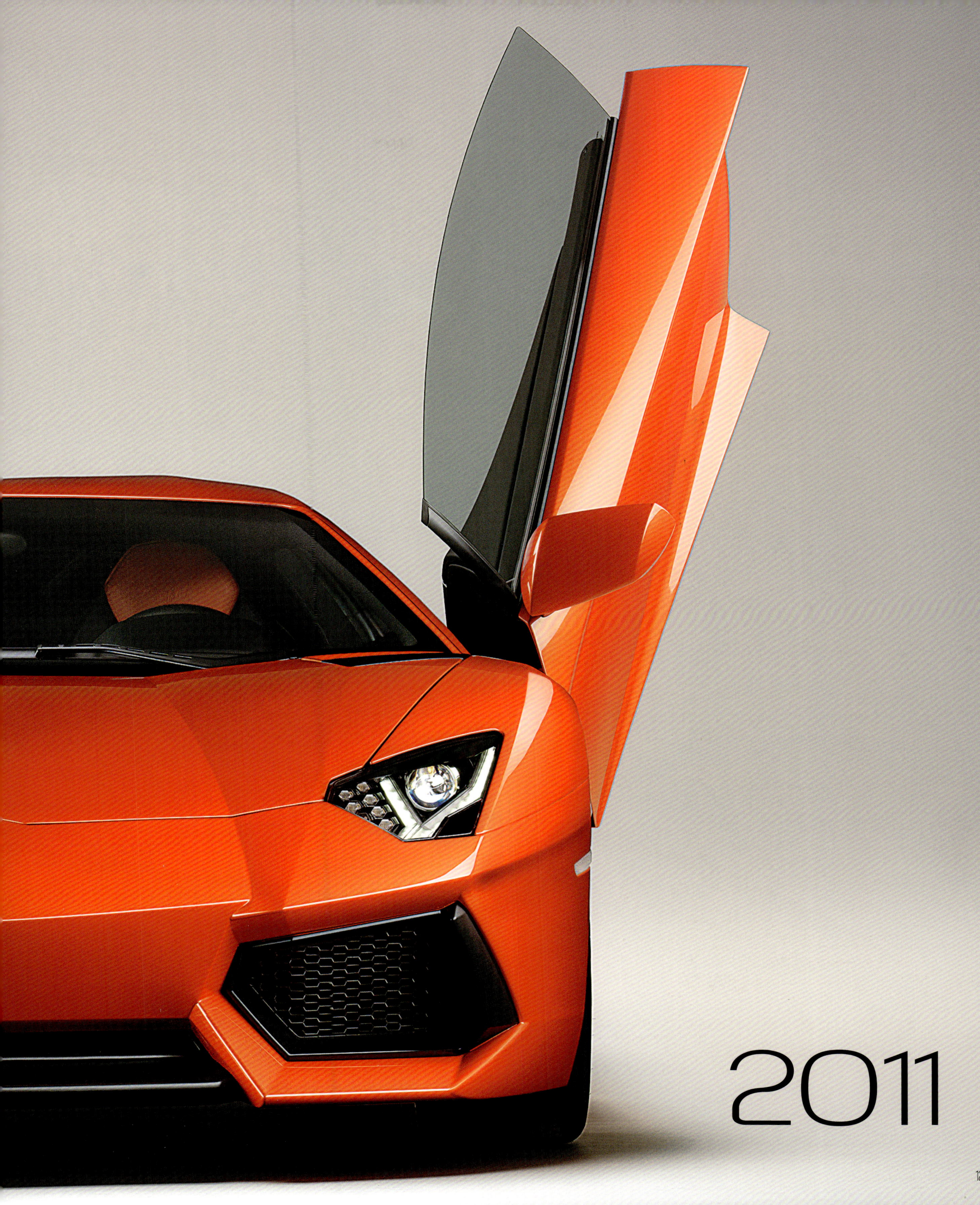

2011

UP CLOSE

Carbon fiber monocoque, push-rod suspension inspired by the world of Formula 1, 6.5-liter (396.65 cu. in.) V12 engine churning out 700 cv (690.5 hp), all-wheel drive, automated gearbox, and a maximum speed of 350 kph (around 217.5 mph). The Lamborghini Aventador debuted at the 2011 Geneva Motor Show and did so while previewing what was to become an essential feature for the marque founded by Ferruccio Lamborghini. "The future of our supercars becomes a reality with the Aventador LP 700-4," declared Stephan Winkelmann, chairman and CEO of Automobili Lamborghini, anticipating the direction taken over the following decade. The Aventador LP 700-4, with its carbon fiber monocoque, then a first for the Emilian supercars, consolidated Lamborghini's leadership in the production and development of composite materials, making the Sant'Agata marque the first company to succeed in producing in-house—and in large numbers—carbon fiber elements of such complexity. The Aventador's carbon fiber monocoque, constructed utilizing diverse Lamborghini patented technologies, was of the integrated type, combining the cockpit cell, floorpan, and roof of

the car in a single structure, guaranteeing particularly high structural rigidity. The personalization of driving styles also evolved together with the Aventador. The three driving modes of the Aventador LP 700-4 in fact offered five gear change styles: three manual (road, sport, and race) and two automatic (road-auto and sport-auto). The interior was also innovative, more luxuriously finished, and more comfortable, with a more extensive range of accessories than the Murciélago.

LP 550-2
VALENTINO BALBONI

A tribute to the legendary test driver, the Lamborghini Gallardo LP 550-2 Valentino Balboni was lighter and exclusively rear-wheel drive. The maximum power output dropped by around 10 cv (9.87 hp); hence the 550-2 designation. This slight fall was compensated by the reduction in weight, which took the overall mass to around 1,380 kilos (3,042 lbs.; 1,500 kg / 3,306 lbs. for the LP560-4). The LP 550-2 Valentino Balboni was capable of sprinting from 0 to 100 kph (0 to 62 mph) in 3.9 seconds, two-tenths more than its all-wheel-drive sister car, topping out at a maximum of 320 kph (198.84 mph). Produced in just 250 examples, all with a numbered plaque signed by Balboni, the car featured a mechanical specification adapted to the new two-wheel-drive configuration, above all in terms of the springing, dampers, anti-roll bars, and tires. Eight colors were available, including Monocerus White, Noctis Black, Ithaca Green, and Borealis Orange, all combined with a white-and-gold stripe running longitudinally from the front hood to the rear spoiler. The same luminous color scheme was applied to the interior, too, where a contrasting white leather center stripe was applied to the black seat upholstery, and the central tunnel was finished in Polar White leather. Taken on by Ferruccio Lamborghini himself in 1967, from 1973, Valentino Balboni tested every Lamborghini prototype and the majority of production cars, from the Countach to the Diablo, the Murciélago, the Gallardo, and the Aventador.

2013

AVENTADOR ROADSTER

In the roadster version of the Aventador, the roof was composed of two elements and made entirely in carbon fiber, representing a further step forward with respect to the Murciélago, which had a canvas roof. This technology guaranteed excellent styling and stiffness while maintaining extreme lightness. Each element in fact weighed less than 6 kilos (13.2 lbs.) and could be stowed in a space created within the luggage compartment when not in use.

VENENO

The 2013 Geneva Motor Show. Once again, Lamborghini stunned both press and public with the presentation of the Veneno, an exclusive few-off model in coupé and roadster forms celebrating the marque's fiftieth anniversary. The Veneno was aggressive, potent, and futuristic, its styling consistent with its performance. Powered by the incredible 6.5-liter (366.65 cu. in.) V12 producing 750 cv (around 740 hp), the Veneno was capable of a maximum speed of 355 kph (220.59 mph) and of sprinting from 0 to 100 kph (0 to 62 mph) in just 2.8 seconds. It was characterized by what were new technical and aerodynamic features for Lamborghini, including the monocoque, the chassis, and the bodywork in carbon fiber; the seven-speed ISR gearbox with five different driving modes; and innovative materials such as Forged Composites and CarbonSkin. At the front, the hood presented a central element connected to the two wheel arches by two wings, generating tremendous downforce. The two vents channeling the air from the front splitter toward the upper body had a hexagonal cut, and the headlight units, characterized by a large vertical Y, anticipated the styling of future features.

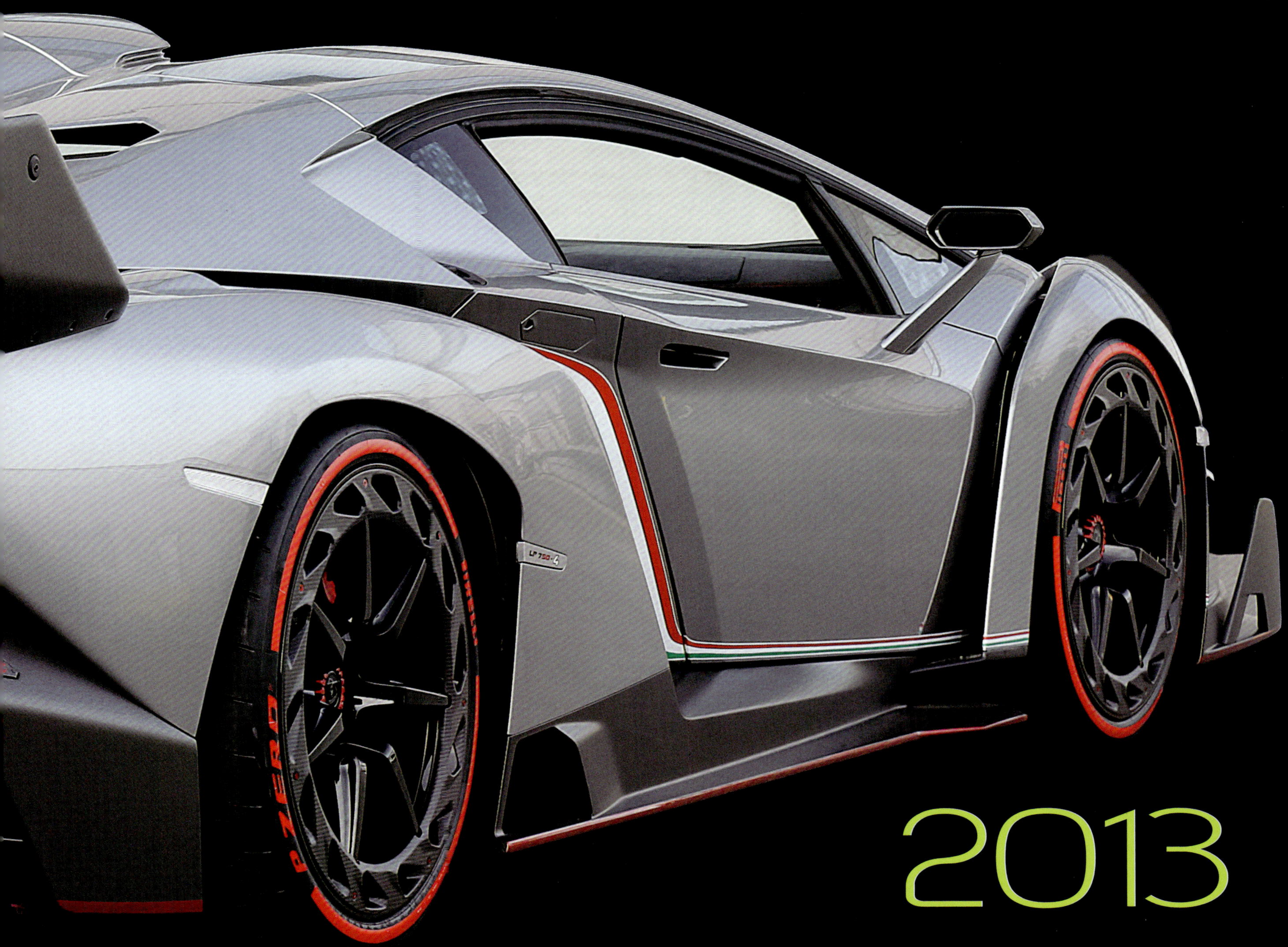

2013

BLANCPAIN
BLANCPAIN
JAKARTA
MAD-CROC
Racing
63
LAMBORGHINI
JAKARTA
PIRELLI
Lamborghini

THE BIRTH OF LAMBORGHINI SQUADRA CORSE

In 2013 the need to create a division at Sant'Agata Bolognese dedicated to the world of competition, with a precisely defined internal structure, was confirmed. This led to the birth that year of Lamborghini Squadra Corse, the point of reference for all the Raging Bull's single-marque championships and a long series of activities that expanded year after year. In fact, Lamborghini Squadra Corse designs and produces in-house the cars destined for its sporting clients. Moreover, it provided those clients the opportunity to develop special personalized projects oriented toward track use. The first one-off in the history of the Sant'Agata Bolognese motorsport department was the SC18 Alston in 2018. This unique car, designed in synergy with the client and the Centro Stile Lamborghini, is fully road legal but conceived prevalently for use on track. It is characterized by extreme aerodynamics, developed specifically for the model and drawing on the Squadra Corse's competition experience. The racing elements start with the hood, with air intakes similar to those of the Huracán GT3 EVO. The flanks instead feature wheel arches, fins, and air scoops inspired by the Huracán Super Trofeo EVO. Again in 2018, twenty-six years since its last Grand Prix, the Minardi M191B returned to the track. Chassis #003, equipped with the Lamborghini V12 LE3512 engine, competed in the 1992 Formula 1 World Championship. This car anticipated Lamborghini Squadra Corse's ability to produce high-performance engines for the world of motorsport.

2013

THE BIRTH OF THE HURACÁN

The 2014 Geneva Motor Show. Stephan Winkelmann revealed to the press the new Lamborghini Huracán, heir to the Gallardo and about to become the best-selling sports car in the history of the models produced at Sant'Agata Bolognese. The Huracán LP610-4 was fitted with a naturally aspirated V10 engine displacing 5.2 liters (317.3 cu. in.) and producing 610 cv (601.76 hp) and 560 Nm of torque. It was fitted with a dual clutch, seven-speed gearbox, and electronically controlled all-wheel drive. The model could reach a top speed of over 325 kph (202 mph) and sprint from 0 to 100 kph (0 to 62 mph) in 3.2 seconds and from 0 to 200 kph (0 to 124 mph) in 9.9 seconds. Created on the basis of a hybrid carbon fiber and aluminium chassis, the Gallardo's styling was characterized by sharp, clean lines, with the lighting entrusted to all-LED units. A virtual instrument panel was featured in the cabin on a 12.3-inch TFT screen. The three driving modes (Strada, Sport, and Corsa—road, sport, and race) could be activated via a selector on the steering wheel. The ANIMA (Adaptive Network Intelligent Management) system acted on the engine, gearbox, all-wheel drive, ESC electronics, active steering, and adaptive suspension. The standard equipment list boasted a braking system with carbon ceramic discs.

2014

HURACÁN LP 610-4 SPYDER

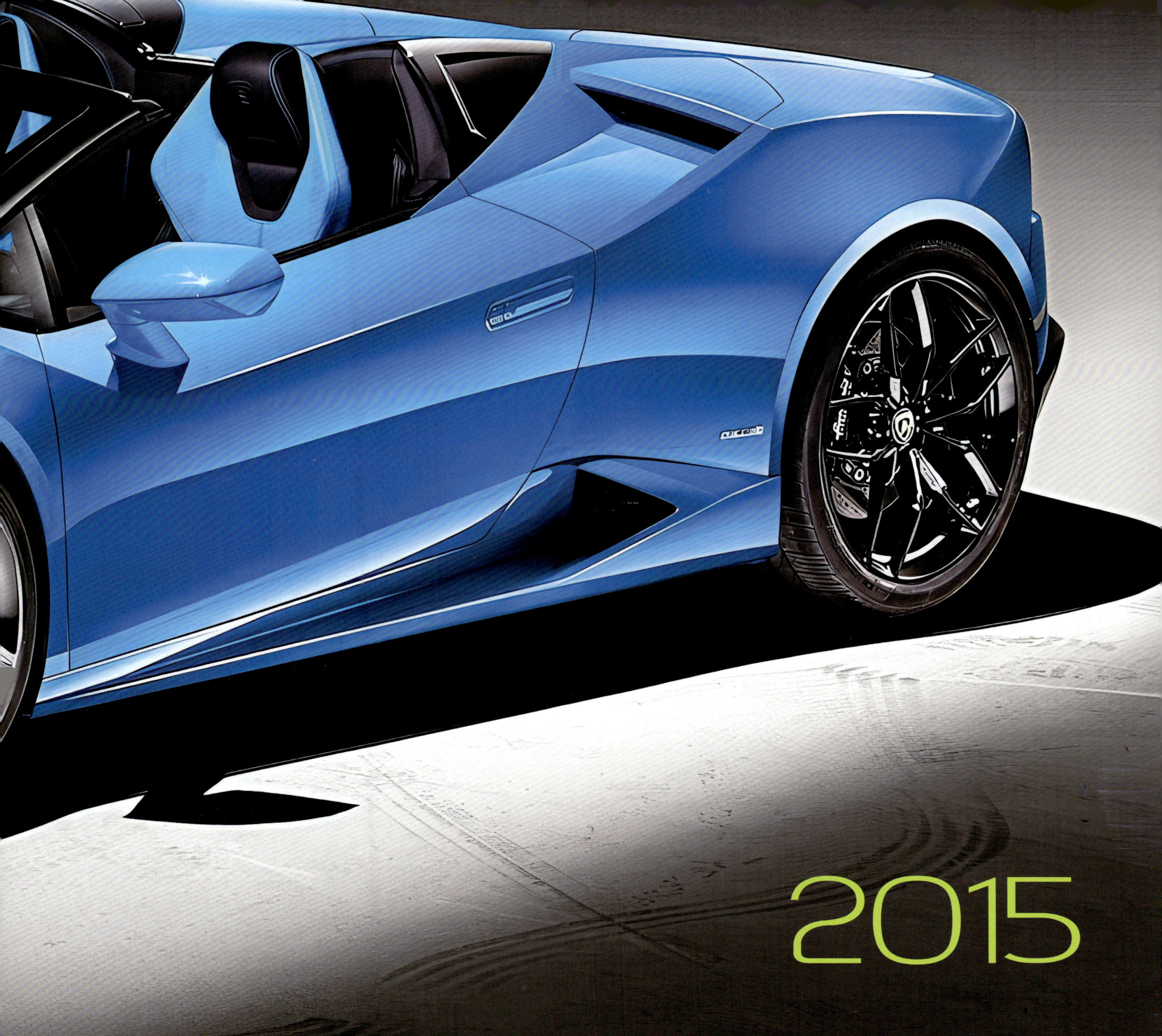

2015

The Huracán Spyder debuted at the Frankfurt Motor Show in 2015, combining the power and performance of the coupé with all the thrills of open-top motoring. The naturally aspirated 5.2-liter (317.3 cu. in.) V12 engine developed a power output of 449 kw / 602.4 hp. The new Huracán LP 610-4 Spyder could sprint from 0 to 100 kph (0 to 62 mph) in just 3.4 seconds and reach a maximum speed of 324 kph (202 mph). The classic Spyder hood was made of lightweight canvas and was actuated by an electrohydraulic mechanism. The car also offered all the new technical innovations of the 2016 model year, including the "cylinder on demand" technology combined with the "stop-and-start" system and a new electronically controlled all-wheel-drive system that further improved its handling. In the best Lamborghini traditions, the heir to the Gallardo also took its name from the world of bullfighting: Huracán was in fact a fighting bull of the Spanish Conte de la Patilla breed that entered the Alicante arena in August 1879. Its indomitable nature made it invincible.

FROM THE THIRD MODEL TO THE ELECTRIC ERA

2015/2029

AUTOMOBILI
LAMBORGHINI

URUS SE
REVUELTO

STEPHAN WINKELMANN OPENS THE PATH TO THE FUTURE

Stephan Winkelmann was born in Berlin on October 18, 1964, and grew up in Rome. He studied political science in Rome and subsequently graduated in Munich. In 1991 he set out on his professional career at a German financial institution before entering the automotive sector, working first at Mercedes-Benz and then at Fiat Auto from 1994 to late 2004, progressing to the position of CEO of Fiat Austria, Switzerland, and Germany. Between 2005 and 2016 he held the position of chairman and CEO of Automobili Lamborghini S.p.A. In March 2016 he was appointed CEO of Quattro GmbH (today Audi Sport GmbH) before joining Bugatti Automobiles S.A.S. as chairman from early 2018 through November 2021. On December 1, 2020, he returned to Lamborghini as chairman and CEO.

Your first memory after joining in 2005?

I've two very clear memories of my arrival at Lamborghini. The first is from January 2005 at the Detroit Motor Show, where I made my first public appearance as chairman and CEO. Martin Winterkorn, then the chairman of Audi AG, wanted to introduce me personally to the company and, not managing to do so at the beginning of January, chose the Lamborghini stand at the American show as the ideal setting for my debut before the press and public. The second was my first actual day at work, when Winterkorn accompanied me to Sant'Agata Bolognese. He introduced me to the managers with a speech in Italian rather than German, a move that raised a few eyebrows.

What were the most important challenges between 2005 and 2016?

The first challenge was to improve the quality standard and the sales figures of the Gallardo. The car did not meet the standards we had in mind, and was struggling to find the right market position. We decided to reduce the production capacity to create greater demand, while at the same time we improved quality and the performance of the V10 engine, rapidly obtaining excellent sales figures. These moves allowed me to understand how, having a strong marque and working on every detail, commercial success would not be slow in arriving. As well as getting to know in depth our team and the markets in which we were active, we worked on the basic product investment and began to create the project for special versions derived from the models in our range. Not just open-top and facelifted versions, but novelties to be launched year by year, all united by painstaking work on the technological innovation offered. It was immediately clear to us that anyone purchasing a Lamborghini wants to make a dream come true. Moreover, as we were still one of the "underdogs," we were able to concentrate on a precise and unequivocal positioning with respect to our competitors and the market. Over the past decade, this has translated—before the arrival of the Urus—into excellent commercial results in the Aventador and Huracán niche markets.

The production of the Urus at Sant'Agata is in fact a source of pride for the company. What can you tell us about the negotiations with the group and with the Italian government?

The idea for a third model arose very quickly, leading us in 2012 to present the Urus concept at the Beijing Motor Show. Its great success assured us that we were on the right path, even though the production of a model such as the Urus would require major investments, a significant increase in the workforce, and a thorough shake-up of the company. First and foremost, we would have to overcome the group's concerns regarding production in Italy, when it would have made economic sense to build the vehicle abroad. We were convinced that the Urus had to be produced at Sant'Agata Bolognese, and thanks in part to the support of the Italian government at the time, we managed to achieve our objective.

Following your experience as CEO of Audi Sport and Bugatti, you returned to Automobili Lamborghini as chairman and CEO. What were your first objectives?

I came back in December 2020 after a very complex period caused by the first phase of the coronavirus pandemic. With the exception of the Urus, the range had begun to feel the passing of the years. Sales figures were satisfactory, but it was important to get new projects up and running. While there were profound uncertainties regarding the economic situation post-COVID, not knowing how the market would have reacted, we were nonetheless very clear regarding our intention to produce a fourth model. Apart from the objectives to be reached, I'm still moved by the memory of the long applause from the staff when I rejoined the company.

In 2021 you announced the "Direzione Cor Tauri" strategy, supported by the most extensive investment plan in the history of Lamborghini. What are the fundamental aspects of this plan?

The Cor Tauri business plan, announced for the first time in 2021 and followed by the most important investment made since the birth of the marque, launched a profound and ongoing investigation into the opportunities and challenges posed by electrification. Challenges that have translated into the start of the hybridization phase in 2023 with the launch of the Revuelto, the first high-performance hybrid supercar or HPEV (high-performance electrified vehicle), followed in 2024 by the debut of the Urus SE plug-in hybrid and the Temerario, powered by the new V8 engine. In addition to the electrification of the range, completed with the all-electric fourth model expected in 2029, the Direzione Cor Tauri plan intends to reduce CO_2 emissions throughout the production cycle by 40 percent per car within 2023 (with respect to 2021). The commitment therefore extends to the whole business, from production to the supply chain and logistics, through to the product use phase, covering the entire lifecycle of the product and involving the entire company in a collective pledge.

In 2023 you surpassed the 10,000-vehicles-delivered threshold for the first time. What should we expect in the future?

Our principal objective remains the margin on the cars and the value of the marque, characteristics that allow us to invest in the future and in technological innovation. This makes it possible to build cars that exceed our clients' dreams, counting on a production capable of ensuring an elevated residual value, and a relatively long waiting list, but in line with the expectations of the future owners.

The renewal of the sports car range has been completed with the Temerario. Is there one aspect or characteristic that has struck you in particular?

We've created a car with all the potential to become an icon. I find the styling exceptional, starting from the front end, from the silhouette—capable of rendering it immediately recognizable, and from the rear end, characterized by a strong personality. To this is added the enormous potential guaranteed by the V8 twin-turbo plug-in hybrid power unit, producing 920 cv (907.5 hp) at 10,000 rpm. In terms of our engines, we have made two maverick choices, retaining the V12 on the Revuelto and fitting the Temerario with an eight- rather than six-cylinder unit, decisions that have been met with the approval of our clients from the launch.

WORK BEGINS ON THE FACTORY EXPANSION

By 2015, more than fifty years had passed since Ferruccio Lamborghini laid the foundation for the factory in Sant'Agata Bolognese, where in 1963 the original building was erected in just eight months. From the 12,000 square meters (around 130,000 sq. ft.) of covered area in 1966, the Emilian plant grew year by year. The first major turning point came after 1998, thanks to the arrival of the Audi group. Early in the new millennium, Lamborghini produced 296 cars and had a workforce of 440 employees. In 2001 the plant was renovated for the first time in many years, with the work involving the construction of a new office building, a two-story museum, and a new research and development area, as well as investments regarding the assembly lines and the staff canteen. The project was completed in August 2001 at a total cost of 155 million euros. On October 25, 2002, it was announced that to celebrate the company's fortieth anniversary, the Centro Stile Lamborghini would be opening in late spring 2023 in a reserved area of the new building that would also house the customer service center dedicated to historic Lamborghinis and the marine engines sector. In 2003 the company was growing fast and occupied an area of 100,000 square meters (1,076,391 sq. ft.), of which 28,900 (311,000 sq. ft.) were covered; produced 1,305 cars; and had 624 employees, 145 of whom were working in the research and development department. In November 2008, work began on the expansion of the finishing department, an area dedicated to the final check of the cars coming off the assembly line, while October of that year saw the opening of the new integrated logistics platform, now located within the Sant'Agata Bolognese plant in a new purpose-built building. The new logistics center covers an area of 11,000 square meters (around 118,500 sq. ft.). 2011 saw the debut of the new Aventador, equipped with an innovative carbon fiber monocoque, designed and produced entirely by the company from Sant'Agata Bolognese, thanks in part to the inauguration of CFK "Lamborghini Carbon Production." The Lamborghini Park was also inaugurated in 2011, while in 2012 a completely new building was constructed to house the prototype development (PSC-Protoshop) and the Pre Series Center, Italy's first energy class A and N-ZEB (Net Zero Emission Building) multiple industrial building. In 2015, Automobili Lamborghini inaugurated the new trigeneration and district heating systems, two of the main projects that allowed the company from Sant'Agata Bolognese to obtain CO_2 neutral certification for the entire plant. In 2018, with the arrival of the third model, the Urus super SUV, whose production at Sant'Agata Bolognese was strongly promoted by Stephan Winkelmann—CEO and chairman of Automobili Lamborghini—and supported by a historic agreement with the Italian government and the Emilia-Romagna region, the factory increased its covered surface area to 160,000 square meters (1,722,225 sq. ft.).

The new production facility comprises the assembly line devoted entirely to Urus, the new finishing department for all Lamborghini models, and the new office building with LEED Platinum certification. A new test track with diverse surfaces specifically for SUVs, a new logistics warehouse, a second trigeneration plant, and the new "Energy Hub" have also been inaugurated. The "Manifattura Lamborghini" production model has been introduced, bringing an innovative and sustainable approach that combines craftsmanship with the most advanced technologies. In 2019 the paint shop for the Urus was inaugurated.

HURACÁN GT3

The first Lamborghini entered in the GT championship, the Huracán GT3, was developed in-house by Squadra Corse and, in its first year, took part in the Blancpain Endurance Series. Featuring a hybrid aluminum–carbon fiber chassis, it was equipped with an FIA-compliant roll cage extending to the rear axle. Several chassis components were modified at the front to ac-

commodate a high-efficiency central radiator for engine cooling. At the rear, modifications were made to improve the location of the gearbox, developed for racing use, while also enhancing the aerodynamics. The bodywork, made of composite materials, and the aerodynamics were designed in collaboration with Dallara Engineering and with the direct support of the engineer Giampaolo Dallara. The rear-wheel-drive Huracán GT3 was fitted with a direct-injection V10 engine based on that of the road-going car and equipped with a Bosch Motorsport control unit managing the data, traction control, gearbox, and TFT display on the car's dashboard.

2015

Lamborghini
BLANCPAIN

HURACÁN LP 620-2 SUPER TROFEO

In terms of the chassis, the extreme lightness of the roll cage extending to the rear axle, weighing just 43 kilos (94.8 lbs.), was of note, as was the exceptional torsional rigidity, improved by 45 percent over the previous Gallardo. The Super Trofeo had a dry weight of 1,270 kilos (2,800 lbs.), distributed according to a 42/58 percent ratio between the front and rear axles. Among the various refinements on the bodywork, which was developed in collaboration with Dallara Engineering, were the quick-release system for attaching the body panels and the adoption of an even more effective engine and gearbox oil cooler. The new Huracán Super Trofeo adopted the direct-injection V10 engine of the road-going car, managed by a MoTeC electronic control unit and delivering a power output of 620 cv (612 hp), which corresponded to an extraordinary weight-to-power ratio of 2.05 kg/cv (4.57 lbs./hp). One major change was the adoption of exclusively rear-wheel drive, as was already the case in racing reserved for GT classes. In addition, the car featured rigid engine mounts on the chassis, a triple-plate clutch, and a specially developed XTrac six-speed sequential gearbox.

2015

CENTENARIO

Presented at the 2016 Geneva Motor Show, the Lamborghini Centenario was created to celebrate the one hundredth anniversary of the birth of the founder of the marque, Ferruccio Lamborghini. It was the first model born under the aegis of Stefano Domenicali, who had been appointed CEO of Automobili Lamborghini in February 2016. A "few-off" produced in just forty examples, twenty coupés and twenty roadsters, the Centenario was powered by the 770 cv (760 hp) naturally aspirated V12 engine, capable of ensuring a 0–100 kph (0–62 mph) sprint in 2.8 seconds, 0–300 kph (0–186.5 mph) in 23.5 seconds, and a top speed in excess of 350 kph (217 mph). The body of the Centenario was made entirely of carbon fiber, as were the monocoque, trim elements, and all other bodywork components. With a dry weight of just 1,520 kilos (3,351 lbs.), the Centenario boasted a power-to-weight ratio of 1.97 kg/cv (4.4 lbs./hp). The car's aerodynamic configuration included an extendable rear spoiler, which could provide more downforce at high speeds. The introduction of rear-wheel steering offered greater stability and agility, while the touchscreen allowed one to interface with the connected infotainment system with Apple CarPlay.

2016

TERZO MILLENNIO

The Terzo Millennio concept car was created by the Centro Stile Lamborghini, led by newly appointed director Mitja Borkert, who had arrived in Sant'Agata Bolognese in 2016 to replace Filippo Perini, in partnership with the Massachusetts Institute of Technology (MIT). The project lent concrete form to the design and technological visions of tomorrow while retaining all the visual appeal, breathtaking performance, and, most importantly, the excitement that characterize every aspect of a Lamborghini.

The goal of the project was to enable Lamborghini to develop the technologies needed to be able to approach the future of the supercar from five different directions: energy storage systems, innovative materials, propulsion systems, visionary design, and driving excitement. A key aspect for a Lamborghini hypercar of the future will be to continue to convey all the excitement of sitting behind the wheel of a true Lamborghini and ensure an all-around driving experience.

The responsiveness of the electric motors, the torque control provided by the all-wheel drive, and the dynamic body control system will enhance that driving experience, propelling it into the third millennium. In particular, the innovative approach toward aerodynamics and lightness will result in new longitudinal and lateral dynamics, hitherto unknown in this combination for electric cars. Among the innovations is the Virtual Cockpit, with driving assistance from a virtual expert.

2017

HURACÁN PERFORMANTE

Presented at the 2017 Geneva Motor Show, the Lamborghini Huracán Performante debuted as the most extreme version of the V10 coupé. The mechanical specification was optimized with respect to the base Huracán but without revolutionizing the project: The naturally aspirated V10, displacing 5,200 cc (317.3 cu. in.), offered around 30 extra horses, for a maximum output of 640 cv (631.36 hp), and an extra 40 Nm of torque, for a maximum of 600 Nm, while retaining the all-wheel-drive system and seven-speed dual-clutch transmission. At the back, the new raised exhausts caught the eye and freed up the lower section for a new diffuser, while the flanks were characterized by the new air intakes and the tricolor stripe on the lower part of the doors. The interior confirmed the Performante's extreme vocation, with the principal instrumentation adopting new graphics according the driving mode adopted. The weight dropped by around 40 kilos (88 lbs.) to 1,382 kilos (3,046.78 lbs.). Among the novelties were the elements in Forged Composite, a material permitting more complex forms to be obtained than with carbon fiber, and it was used for the spoilers, the engine cover, the rear bumper, and the diffuser. Also making its debut was the Aerodinamica Lamborghini Attiva (ALA) technology, developed to exploit downforce in relation to performance without penalizing aerodynamic efficiency. The flaps on the front spoiler and at the rear were in fact equipped with moving parts actuated by integrated electric motors controlled by the inertial platform (LPI—Lamborghini Piattaforma Inerziale), which permitted the incidence to be varied in less than 500 milliseconds through inputs from the onboard devices.

2017

URUS

2017

UP CLOSE

Presented on December 4, 2017, the Lamborghini Urus created a new niche market, specifically that of maxi SUVs with supercar performance. If we combed the price lists, we might have found models with power outputs worthy of a supercar, but what the Sant'Agata marque brought was driving pleasure and a series of innovations never previously seen on a high-wheel vehicle. Thanks to the 4.0-liter (244 cu. in.) V8 engine, the Urus sprints from 0 to 100 kph (0 to 62 mph) in 3.6 seconds and reaches a top speed of 305 kph (almost 190 mph). Thanks to the Anima selector, it can also switch smoothly from the kerbs of the track to off-road mud. The dimensions of the Lamborghini Urus rightfully place it within the maxi SUV segment, as confirmed by its length of 5,112 millimeters (16.8 feet). However, thanks to its low height of 1,638 millimeters (5.37 feet), the new model from the Raging Bull presents dynamic styling that makes it seem more compact than its actual dimensions. The design brings references from the past to the road, including the kind of diagonals first seen on the Countach. At the front, the horizontally set lighting units, with LED lamps in the typical Lamborghini Y-shape, are conspicuous features, while at the rear, the strong lines of the tailgate stand out. The hexagonal wheel arches, both front and rear, are an important design detail inspired by the LM002 and the Countach and accommodate alloy wheels in 21-, 22-, and 23-inch sizes. There is no lack of space on board the new Lamborghini Urus. Thanks to the wheelbase of more than 3 meters (9.8 feet), the cabin can comfortably accommodate up to five people, four if single rear seats are chosen. When you open the automatic, foot-operated tailgate, you are faced with a 616-liter (21.75 cu. ft.) luggage compartment that can be expanded to 1,596 liters (56.36 cu. ft.) by folding down

the rear seats. Moving on to infotainment, we find the Lis III system with connected voice control capable of recognizing commands handling music, calls, and text messages, with an extensive list of information displayed on the instrument panel. In addition to the two touchscreens, the fully customizable TFT instrumentation stands out, which when we select the "Corsa" mode via the Anima selector presents us with overtly racing-style graphics. Built on the MLB Evo platform, the Urus is powered by the 4.0-liter (244 cu. in.) V8 Biturbo engine delivering 650 cv (641.2 hp) and 850 Nm of maximum torque available at 2,250 rpm. Despite its size, its weight has has been con-

tained below 2,200 kilos (4,850 lbs.), with a weight-to-power ratio of 3.38 kg/cv (7.56 lbs./hp). Also contributing to driving pleasure is the rear-wheel steering system, introduced with the Aventador S and available at all times. The rear steering angle can vary by up to ±3 degrees, depending on the speed of the car and the driving mode selected. The braking system features standard carbon-ceramic discs (CCB) measuring 440 x 40 millimeters (17.3 x 1.6 inches) at the front, with ten-pot calipers and 370 x 30 millimeters (14.6 x 1.2 inches) at the rear. The character of the car can be changed via the so-called Tamburo or Drum, the selector located below the climate control screen. The Anima selector allows us to choose between Strada, Sport, Corsa, and Neve (road, sport, race, and snow) driving dynamics. As an option, two further modes are also available for off-road driving: Terra and Sabbia (terrain and sand).

2017

INSIDE THE NEW FACTORY

With the arrival of the Urus, the Sant'Agata Bolognese marque had to expand in terms of production capacity, staff numbers, and technology and built a factory 4.0. The birth of the first Lamborghini SUV, supported by an overall investment of more than 700 million euros, translated into a 100 percent increase in the productive area, passing from 80,000 to almost 160,000 square meters (from over 860,000 to around 1,722,225 sq. ft.). One of the most interesting aspects of the expansion concerned the timescale, with the increase to 150,00 square meters (1,614,586 sq. ft.) thanks to the creation of the new assembly line dedicated to the Urus, the new paint department for all models, the dedicated test track for the SUVs, the logistics store, a second tri-generation plant, the office building with LEED Platinum certification, and the new centralized energy vector production hub. All this was possible in just eighteen months thanks to the efforts of 3,600 outside workers. The utmost attention was paid to technological innovation, and the dedicated Urus assembly line is characterized by an industry 4.0 approach, integrating new production processes with the work of the Lamborghini staff. Baptized as "Manifattura Lamborghini," the line rests on four fundamental principles: craftsmanship, skills and specialization, ergonomics and safety, and production process. This different approach brought innovations to the manufacturing process, which included collaborative robots flanking the workers to improve ergonomics and the performance of high-quality, repetitive tasks such as underbody bolting, windshield bonding, and wheel mounting. Greater digitalization has also been introduced through touchscreen devices and the presence of AGVs (automatic guided vehicles) for transporting cars and materials. Naturally, great attention has been paid to manual operations, increasing both the level of personalization and the qualitative standards. Added to this long list of innovations is the 10,000 square meters (107,639 sq. ft.) of the new paint shop. The first SUV produced by Lamborghini has contributed to the expansion of the total workforce to over 1,500 people, double the number of workers employed ten years previously.

2017

EXPLORING ICELAND WITH THE URUS: LAMBORGHINI EXPERIENCE

A journey of almost 1,000 kilometers (621 miles) at the wheel of the Urus, the first SUV produced by Lamborghini, exploring the appeal of Iceland, with its lava fields expanding as far as the eye can see, glaciers that move before our eyes, and lunar landscapes. Iceland is a magical place. In less than 100 kilometers (60 miles or so), it is capable of taking you through all the seasons, from the sun that makes the moss on the mountains glow to a violent snowfall. Our adventure in the land discovered by the Vikings begins at the Blue Lagoon. Aboard the Urus, we skirt Lake Kleifarvatn, a deep basin of volcanic origin, the bottom of which legend has it is home to a worm-like monster as big as a whale. Carefully following the track in the sand—Icelanders are very environmentally conscious, and off-roading on unmarked paths is prohibited—we arrive a few meters from the ocean. From here, we set off for one of Iceland's most characteristic places: the black glacier of Kötlujökull. To reach it, I set the Anima selector to Earth, making the Urus perfect for off-road driving and tackling fords and challenging passages. In practice, the different modes radically change the character of the Emilian SUV, transforming it from a vehicle capable of lapping circuits at high speed into a true off-roader.

AVENTADOR SVJ

Super Veloce Jota: This is the origin of the acronym SVJ, a version of the Lamborghini Aventador capable of taking the title of world's fastest production car on the historic Nürburgring-Nordschleife circuit in Germany, having completed the 20.6-kilometer (12.8-mile) lap in just 6 minutes, 44 seconds, and 9.7 tenths. Accredited with a power output of 770 cv (740 hp) and a 0–100 kph (0–62 mph) time of just 2.8 seconds, the Aventador SVJ boasted features such as four-wheel steering, while in order to improve roadholding and performance, Lamborghini Active Aerodynamics 2.0 was introduced along with improved second-generation LDVA (Lamborghini Dinamica Veicolo Attiva). The Lamborghini-patented ALA system, introduced for the first time on the Huracán Performante, became ALA 2.0 on the Aventador SVJ, for which it was recalibrated to take into account the car's greater lateral accelerations. The design of the air intakes and the aerodynamic ducts was also redefined. Produced in 900 examples and sold from 2019, the SVJ represented the ultimate expression of the Aventador that could also be used on track.

2018

LAMBORGHINI HURACÁN EVO

An evolution of the model launched in 2014, the Lamborghini Huracán EVO was so much more than a classic mid-career restyling, to the extent that it presented a long list of innovations, most of which were invisible to the naked eye. In terms of styling, the most significant changes were concentrated at the rear, while to a less-than-attentive eye, the front end remained virtually identical to the model it replaced. The cabin gained a large, vertically oriented touchscreen via which the new human-machine interface

(HMI) could be managed. Beneath the engine cover was the 5.2-liter (317.3 cu. in.) V12; derived from the unit fitted to the Huracán Performante and combined with a new, lightweight exhaust system, it delivered a maximum power output of 640 cv (631 hp) at 8,000 rpm and maximum torque of 600 Nm at 6,500 rpm. The revised aerodynamics, which included the front splitter with an integrated wing, improved the balance and efficiency of the car and increased engine cooling by 16 percent. Another novelty came in the form of the Lamborghini Dinamica Veicolo Integrata (integrated vehicle dynamics system, LDVI): a central processing unit, combined with the four-wheel steering, that controls every aspect of the car's handling, integrating dynamic systems and set up to anticipate the driver's actions and demands, translating them into improved driving dynamics. The LPI acronym instead identifies the Lamborghini Inertial Platform, a network of acceleration and gyroscopic sensors positioned in correspondence with the car's center of gravity, which on the EVO had evolved into the 2.0 version. Thanks to a new advanced control system—combined with all-wheel drive and torque vectoring—traction could be directed to a single wheel on the basis of the conditions. Track day enthusiasts could use the touchscreen to access an optional twin-camera telemetry system with advanced recording and data analysis functions.

2018

SIÁN FKP 37

The Lamborghini Sián made its debut at the Frankfurt Motor Show in 2019. The first hybrid supercar to be produced in Sant'Agata, the Sián added the initials FKP 37 in honor of Ferdinand Karl Piëch, born in 1937, who in 1998 played a key role in the acquisition of Automobili Lamborghini by Audi, of which he was chairman of the Executive Board from 1993 to 2002. Combining an internal combustion and an electric motor to produce 819 cv (807.94 hp), the debut Sián FKP 37 boasted the lowest power-to-weight ratio of any V12-powered car and, using Pirelli P Zero tires, was capable of sprinting from 0 to 100 kph (0 to 62 mph) in less than 2.8 seconds, with a maximum speed of over 350 kph (217.48 mph). New features on the Lamborghini Sián FKP 37 include the world-first use of a supercapacitor in a mild-hybrid configuration.

2019

ON TRACK WITH THE HURACÁN EVO

The sun is setting, the 495 spotlights are blazing, the wind is blowing the sand onto the asphalt, and ahead of me, I have the more than 5 kilometers (3 miles) of the Al Sakhir circuit. I'm in Bahrain to drive the new Lamborghini Huracán EVO, and as I wait to exit the pit lane, I mentally review the new features of the latest model from Sant'Agata Bolognese. A 5.2-liter (317.3 cu. in.), naturally aspirated V10 engine derived from the Huracán Performante, 640 cv (631.36 hp), a top speed of over 325 kph (202 mph), four-wheel steering, all-wheel drive, a connected environment, and technology capable of sensing the driver's choices. The list of changes with respect to the 2014 Huracán goes beyond mere restyling, with the Emilian engineers having focused on increased performance on the road, combined with an ease of use never previously seen on a Raging Bull supercar. The new EVO, or Evoluzione, has become tremendously fast, easy to drive, and versatile thanks to the driving modes available via the Anima selector on the steering wheel. Choosing among Strada, Sport, and Corsa radically modifies the new Lamborghini's character, transforming it from a comfortable supercar for everyday use to the ideal vehicle for improving lap times when taking to the track. In terms of styling, the new design is performance oriented, starting with the revised aerodynamics, which improve the car's balance. While at the front, the novelties focus on the splitter with an integrated wing, at the rear there is a new double-height spoiler and a new extractor to increase downforce and overall balance. With regard to the driving dynamics, the work has been even more extensive, with the introduction of a series of new features never seen on a supercar in this segment. The revamped Huracán, in fact, is capable of anticipating the driver's actions and needs, thanks to the Lamborghini Integrated Vehicle Dynamics (LDVI) system, a central processing unit coupled to the four-wheel steering that controls every aspect of the car's handling, integrating dynamic systems and set up to anticipate the driver's actions and needs, translating them into the optimum driving dynamics. This is possible thanks to the processing unit, which evaluates and recalculates every 20 milliseconds every parameter of the car, with components such as the 2.0 inertial platform, four-wheel steering, torque vectoring, improved dynamic steering, and LMR 2.0 magnetorheological suspension work in unison to guarantee the utmost performance. Completing the list of new features is the new human-machine interface (HMI), which replaced the old Audi-style infotainment system in favor of an 8.4-inch touchscreen. Positioned in the central tunnel, above the start button, it makes the EVO truly connected and features full control of the car, gesture controls, online navigation, Apple CarPlay connectivity, and an optional telemetry system with advanced recording functions, data analysis, and two cameras. Now, however, it's time to take to the track. Thanks in part to the lines demonstrated by the Lamborghini instructor in front of me, I drive around the track created to host Formula 1 at a speed I could never have imagined, with the Huracán EVO following my every impulse and confirming its predictive side. The aspirated V10 plays a true symphony, and in Sport mode I even allow myself some theatrical drifting. Switching to Corsa mode, everything becomes faster, and I thank the talents of the carbon-ceramic system at every braking point.

HURACÁN EVO RWD SPYDER

As with the closed coupé version, the Lamborghini Huracán EVO RWD Spyder brings to the road such features as four-wheel steering centrally managed by the Lamborghini Integrated Vehicle Dynamics (LDVI) system, version 2.0 of the Lamborghini Inertial Platform (LPI), and new connectivity with an 8.4-inch touchscreen and connected environment. In stylistic terms, the new front bumper provides improved aerodynamic efficiency through the front splitter and enlarged air intakes. Eye-catching features at the rear include the new wing and the two tailpipes of the new sports exhaust, located high in the bumper unit. When closed, the lightweight soft top blends perfectly into the car's silhouette, while when open it disappears into a space designed for maximum efficiency. The roll bars are retractable and deploy automatically. Regardless of the position of the soft top, the driver can operate the rear screen electronically. At the touch of a button on the central tunnel, the lightweight, electro-hydraulically actuated soft top opens in just seventeen seconds at speeds

of up to 50 kph (31 mph). When the soft top is lowered, two body-colored fins emerge from the compartment toward the seat backs and, once in place, extend the roofline toward the rear. An integrated duct between the fins reduces turbulence above the passenger compartment when driving with the hood down. In the engine bay, the 5.2-liter (317.3 cu. in.), naturally aspirated V10 from the coupé delivers 640 cv (631.36 hp, 470 kW) at 8,000 rpm and 600 Nm of torque at 6,500 rpm. With a dry weight of 1,542 kilograms (3,399.5 lbs.), the car achieves a weight-to-power ratio of 2.41 kg/cv (5.384 lbs./hp) and is capable of propelling the car from 0 to 100 kph (0 to 62 mph) in 3.1 seconds and from 0 to 200 kph (0 to 124 mph) in 9.3 seconds. The braking distance from 100 kph (62 mph) to a complete stop is just 32.2 meters (105.64 feet), while the top speed is 325 kph (202 mph).

2020

ESSENZA SCV12

A true hypercar, built to ensure ultimate performance on the track, free of the limitations dictated by international regulations. The new Essenza SCV12, the first car completely designed by Lamborghini Squadra Corse and styled by the Centro Stile at Sant'Agata. Produced in just forty examples, at a price of 2.6 million euros, this is a hypercar designed for wealthy enthusiasts, willing to sign six-figure checks to drive the most powerful, naturally aspirated 12-cylinder engine ever developed by Lamborghini on the track. The power output, in fact, exceeds 830 cv (818.8 hp) thanks

to the contribution of dynamic supercharging at high speeds. The exhaust tailpipes, designed in collaboration with Capristo, reduce back pressure, improving performance and emphasizing the engine's unique sound. The six-speed Xtrac gearbox is located transversely on the rear axle and drives the rear wheels only, the push-rod rear suspension is mounted directly on the transmission assembly, and the weight-to-power ratio is 1.66 kg/cv (around 3.7 lbs./hp), thanks to the unprecedented carbon fiber monocoque chassis and the absence of a steel rollcage. Specific Pirelli slick tires mounted on 19-inch magnesium rims at the front and 20-inch rims at the rear complete the picture, with a braking system developed by Brembo Motorsport. The styling of the Essenza SCV12 is the result of the creative work of the Lamborghini Centro Stile, responsible for the looks of all the racing cars from Sant'Agata Bolognese since the foundation of Squadra Corse. The essential character of the car is emphasized by the bodywork structure, composed of just three elements to allow rapid replacement when needed during pit stops. The aerodynamics ensure a level of efficiency and downforce superior to that of a GT3 car, with a value of 1,200 kilograms (2,645.5 lbs.) at 250 kph (155.34 mph).

ON TRACK WITH THE ESSENZA SCV12

"The suit's in box number six, where you'll find all you need to get on board. After changing, Emanuele Pirro will be waiting for the technical briefing." So begins the Lamborghini Essenza SCV12 test drive, with the car ready to show its full potential over the 4 kilometers (2.48 miles) of the Vallelunga circuit. Rather than a normal test drive, I am about to experience what it is like to be one of the forty lucky and wealthy owners, ready and willing to sign a check for over 2.6 million euros to drive a hypercar of a kind never previously seen in Sant'Agata Bolognese. This is no special version derived from the Aventador, but the technological manifesto of Lamborghini's conception of what is the ultimate expression of the naturally aspirated V12 in combination with a body born out of painstaking work in the wind tunnel. The Essenza SCV12, the acronym indicating design and production by Lamborghini Squadra, is a blank-sheet design born with the aim of achieving the optimum performance on the road combined with an ease of use suitable even for gentleman drivers. In fact, the Emilian hypercar was created without any specific regulations or homologation requirements in mind, introducing for the first time in the world such features as the carbon fiber monocoque chassis approved by the FIA as a replacement for the traditional roll bar. All this is offered within the exclusive Essenza SCV12 Club, with the Raging Bull marque offering an all-inclusive service ranging from track days attended by the Squadra Corse team, to the management of the car with the possibility of storage at Sant'Agata in the new hangar and participation in dedicated events. Now it's time for the technical briefing, with an exceptional tutor in the form of five-time 24 Hours of Le Mans winner Emanuele Pirro, who reminds us how the power output exceeds 830 cv (818.8 hp) thanks to dynamic supercharging, the six-speed Xtrac gearbox combined with rear-wheel drive, the push-rod rear suspension mounted directly on the transmission, the weight-to-power ratio of 1.66 kg/cv (around 3.7 lbs./hp), and the record-breaking aerodynamics guaranteeing a downforce value of 1,200 kilograms (2,645.5 lbs.) at 250 kph (155.34 mph). This initial introduction is followed by the most important part; namely, advice on how to actually use the car. The new Formula 1–style steering wheel is a riot of knobs, buttons, and adjustments that can change the soul and character of the car according to the track to be negotiated and the driver's abilities. Now, however, it is time to find out how the new Essenza SCV12 performs, obviously after strapping on my helmet attached to the Hans collar. The experience organized by Lamborghini immediately turns me into a driver. As soon as I get into the car, the mechanics adjust my seatbelts and driving position, while Pirro shows me how to change the settings on the steering wheel to vary the power available or the intervention of the differential. The track engineer gives the go-ahead and I leave the pits, not thinking about the value of the car, but concentrating instead on the reactions of the Pirelli slicks and the braking force of the Brembo carbon-ceramic system. The first five laps are all about caution and learning about what is a true four-wheeled spaceship; I'm helped, however, by the car's general ease of handling, so much so that I find confirmation of Pirro's statement: "The car adapts to the driver's demands." The exhaust system, developed in collaboration with Capristo, provides the kind of sonic thrills that are increasingly rare in the world of motorsport as I speed through the Vallelunga corner. In the second track session, I keep Pirro's advice in mind and manage to knock a couple of seconds off my lap time.

LAMBORGHINI ESSENZA SCV12 CLUB

The Lamborghini Essenza SCV12 Club, a program created for the forty lucky owners of Essenza SCV12s, was born with one goal in mind: the creation of an exclusive club offering access to special programs allowing you to drive your hypercar on some of the world's greatest circuits. Membership of the prestigious club comprises storage in a new, specially built hangar in Sant'Agata Bolognese, with each car placed in a customized garage to which are added dedicated services, such as a webcam allowing customers to monitor their cars around the clock via an app. In addition, the facility houses TecnoBody's "Lamborghini Squadra Corse Drivers Lab," offering physical training with programs similar to those followed by the Lamborghini works drivers. In addition to the events

organized directly by Lamborghini, membership of the Essenza SCV12 Club also brings the possibility of a series of customized activities such as choices of track, period and driving schedule, door-to-door car logistics, an individual driving coach, technical briefing, a dedicated engineer for telemetry and configuration, a personal team of mechanics, hospitality, concierge services for accommodation and transfers, and an on-track spare parts service. There is a long list of circuits used by the Essenza SCV12 Club, including Spa-Francorchamps, Paul Ricard, Nürburgring, Barcelona, Imola, and Vallelunga.

HURACÁN STO

Super Trofeo Omologata: that is to say, a road-legal Lamborghini Huracán racing car. The STO is powered by the 640 cv (631.36 hp), naturally aspirated V10 driving the rear wheels through a seven-speed dual-clutch gearbox. Closely based on the racing cars, among many other features it boasts a new rear wing borrowed from the Huracán Super Trofeo EVO and a striking NACA duct integrated into the rear wing that acts as an air intake for the engine. Unveiled on the day of the appointment of Stephan Winkelmann, who returned in November 2020 to lead Automobili Lamborghini, the STO embodies the principle that Lamborghini design always

2020

STO

Lamborghini
HURACÁN
STO

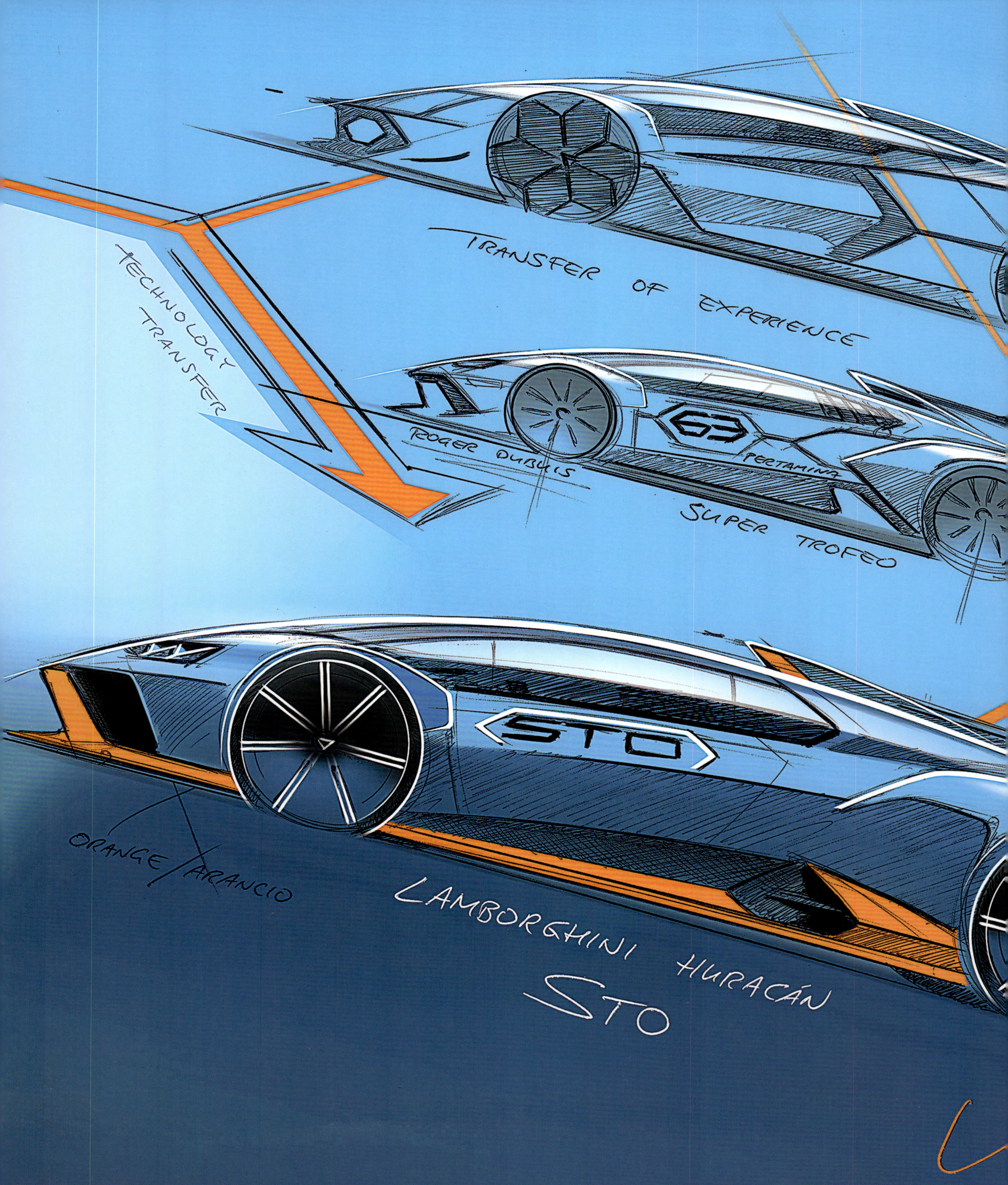
TRANSFER OF EXPERIENCE
TECHNOLOGY TRANSFER
ROGER DUBUIS
PERTAMINA
SUPER TROFEO
STO
ORANGE/ARANCIO
LAMBORGHINI HURACÁN
STO

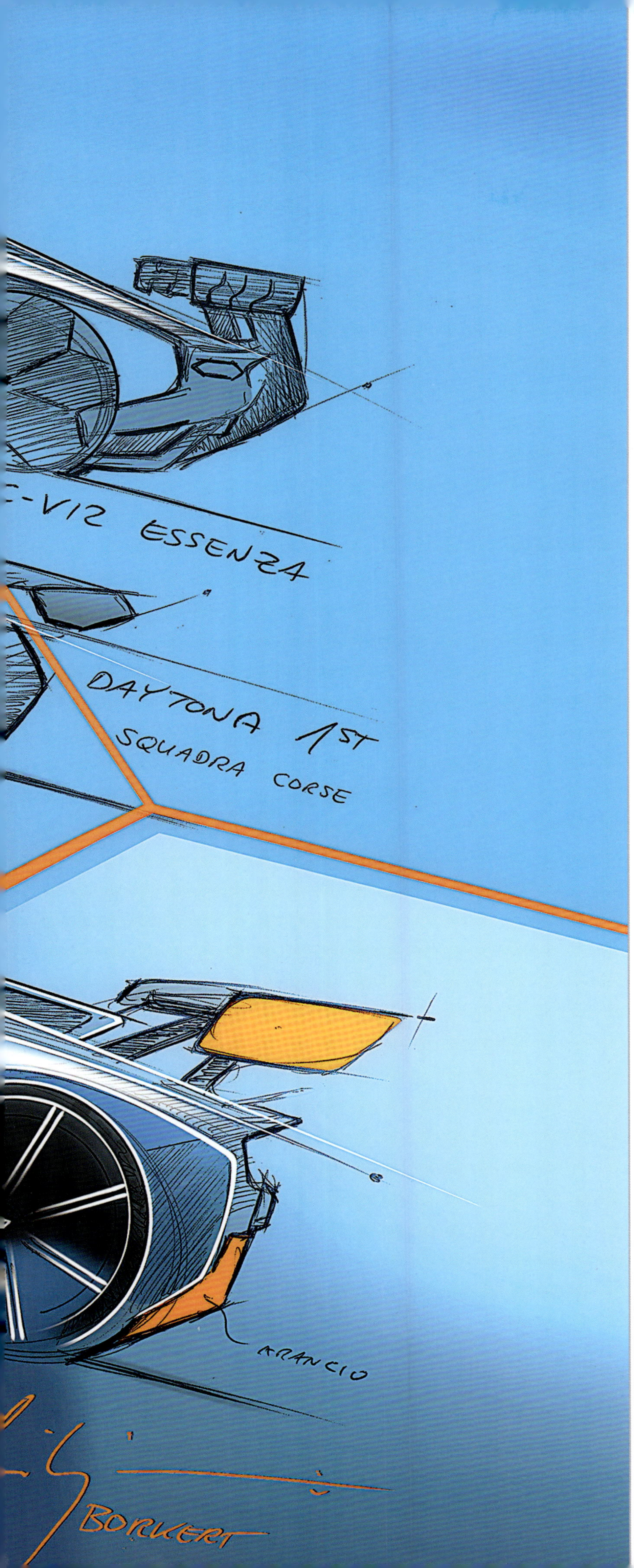

follows function: a principle all the more valid in a road-legal car inspired by competition machinery. Another fundamental aspect of the design process was the quest for lightness. The extensive use of carbon fiber and composite materials means the STO tips the scales at 1,339 kilograms (2,952 lbs.), a full 43 kilograms (94.8 lbs.) less than the already light Huracán Performante. The STO is truly a road-legal racing car. Features such as the increased track width, stiffer suspension bushings, Lamborghini-specific anti-roll bars and MagneRide 2.0 suspension, an Akraprovic exhaust with titanium valves, new engine mapping (STO, Trofeo and Pioggia or Rain modes), and specific Bridgestone Potenza tires all combine to provide benchmark performance. Climb aboard and you will notice the extensive use of carbon fiber: from the sports seats to the Alcantara and Lamborghini Carbonskin upholstery, the carpet replaced with carbon fiber mats and lightweight door panels. Infotainment is provided by the Apple CarPlay–compatible HMI system with a touchscreen, while there is also a fully connected telemetry system capable of monitoring and recording performance on the track and analyzing the data via the Lamborghini Unica app.

LAMBORGHINI SC20

A one-off with a V12 engine designed by Lamborghini Squadra Corse, the SC20 is a track-legal open-top car for road use. The first open special designed by the Sant'Agata Bolognese motorsport department and styled by the Centro Stile Lamborghini, the SC20 was created at the behest of a customer who was involved in the project from the first drawings. A sartorial approach was taken to the production of a supercar with an impressive 770 cv (760 hp) produced by the naturally aspirated 6.5-liter (396.65 cu. in.) V12, transmitted to the asphalt through the four steered wheels. In keeping with Squadra Corse's signature style, the exterior of the SC20 sports a Cepheus Blue detailing over a Fu White base. Further confirmation of the car's sporty character came from the interior, in a combination of Cosmus Black and Leda White that sets off the numerous carbon fiber details.

2020

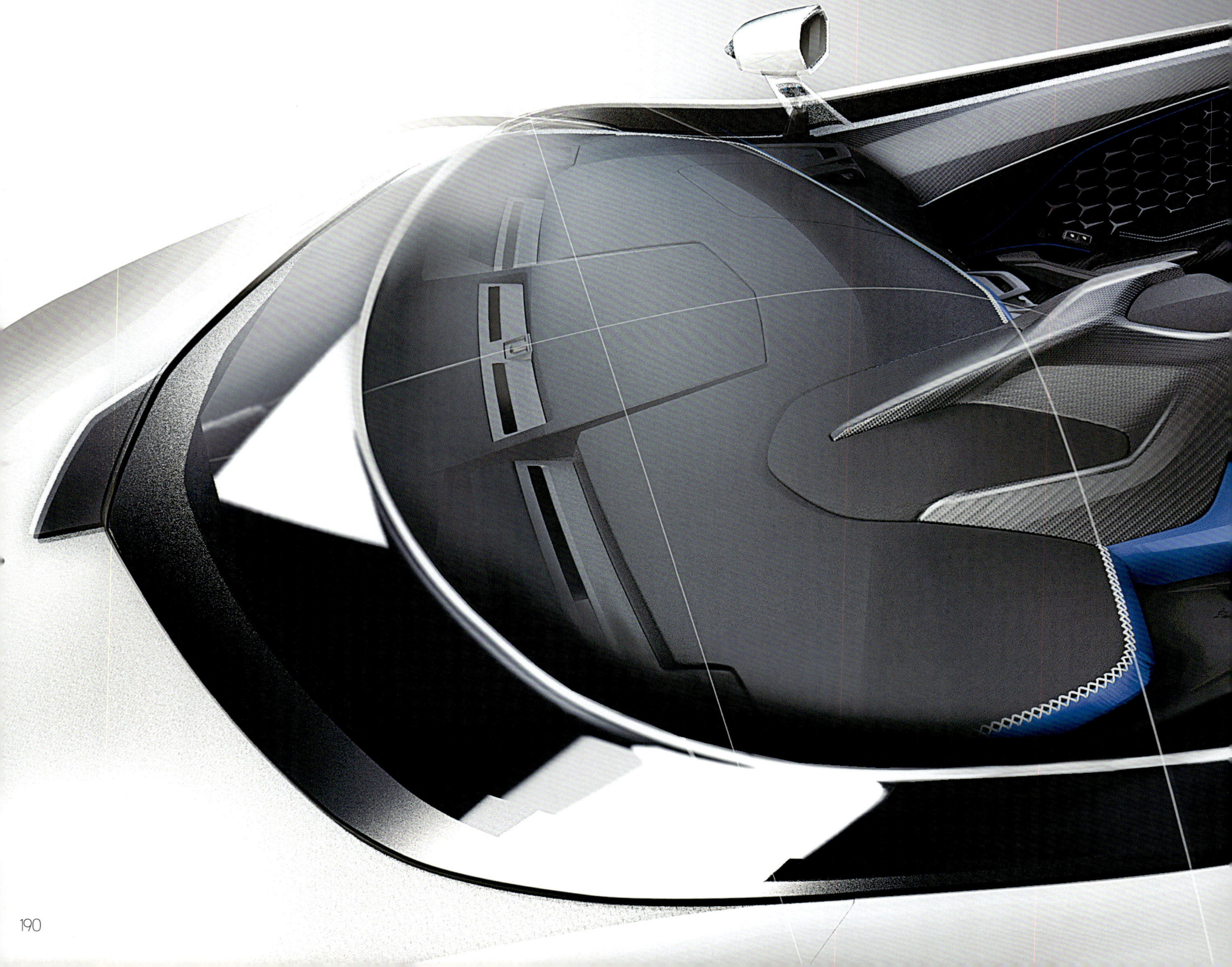

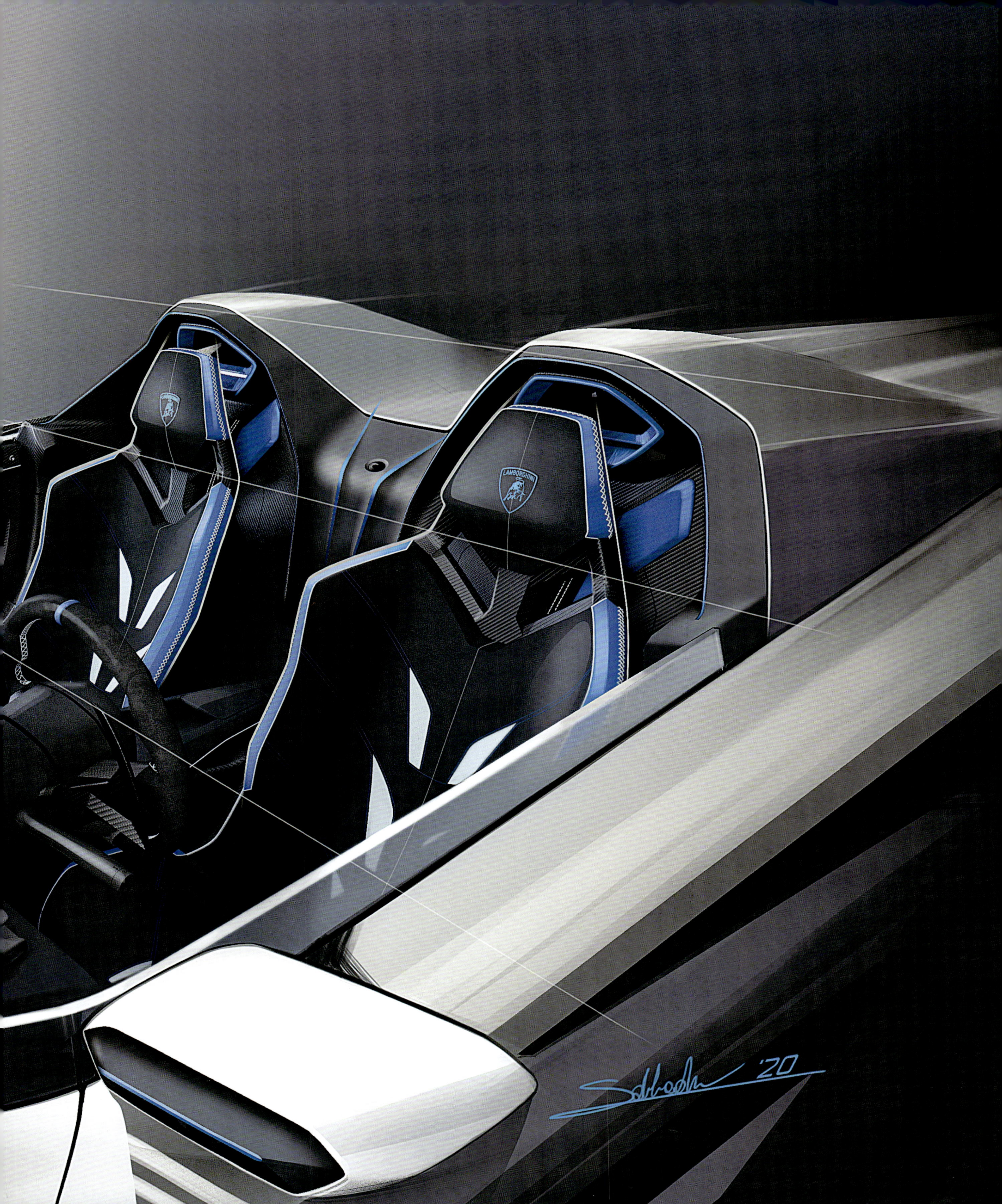
LAMBORGHINI
'20

HURACÁN SUPER TROFEO EVO2

Created by Lamborghini Squadra Corsa, from a stylistic point of view the Huracán Super Trofeo EVO2 takes to the extreme the design of the previous generation, anticipating motifs that will appear on the road cars over the years to come. The front end was radically modified, now characterized by new high-intensity, full-LED lighting clusters with a hexagonal design and an "omega" lip that links the carbon

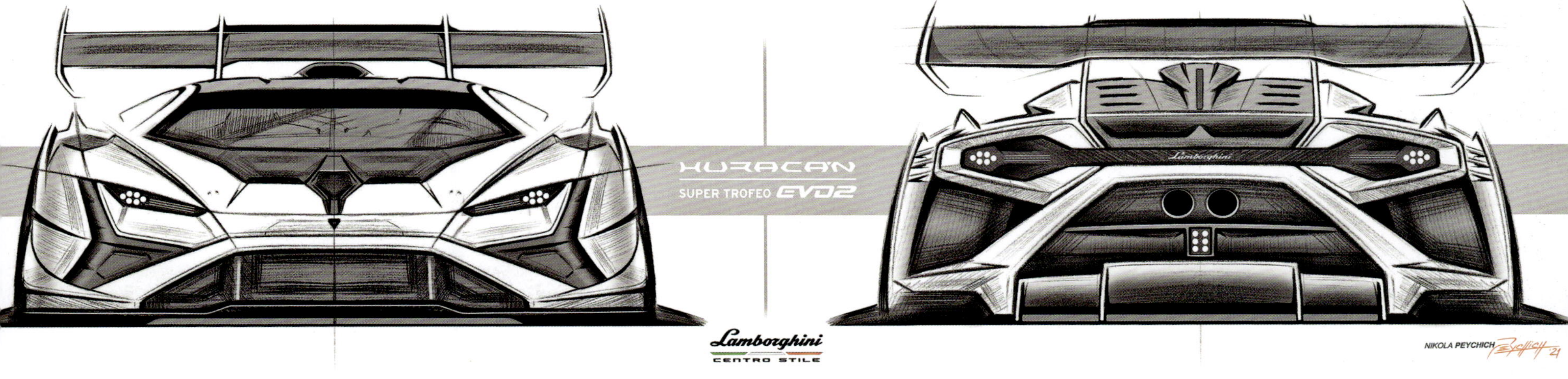

fiber fins and emphasizes the stylistic link with the Huracán STO. The "air curtain" intakes are also new and optimize the drag value and air flows, ensuring they remain attached to the flanks. The rear end, characterized by the large carbon fiber wing, combines a minimalist style with an elevated perception of lightness. The frames of the new LED lighting clusters pay tribute to the styling of the Countach.

The car is powered by the 5.2-liter (317.3 cu. in.) V10 producing 620 cv (611.63 hp) and mated to the Xtrac six-speed sequential gearbox driving the rear wheels. There are also changes to the braking system, designed and developed by Squadra Corse. The front discs in steel have been enlarged from 380 millimeters (15 inches) to 390 millimeters (15.4 inches), and the new calipers can take new pads, with a greater surface area, to optimize performance and durability. The modifications also concern numerous bodywork components, such as the sill covers and the rear aerodynamic appendages, with carbon fiber materials being used instead of plastic materials.

AVENTADOR LP 780-4 ULTIMAE

2021

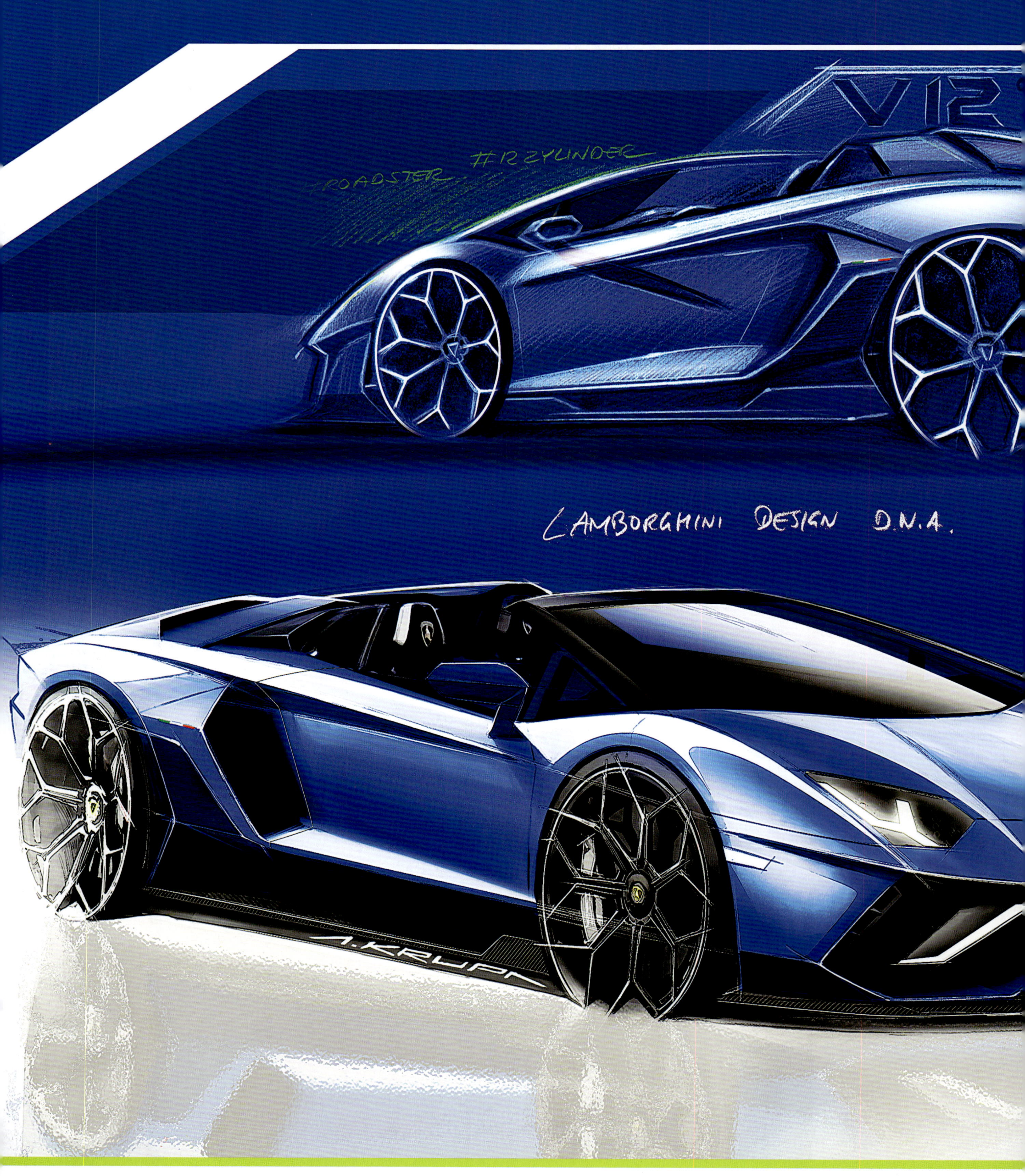
V12
#12ZYLINDER
#ROADSTER
LAMBORGHINI DESIGN D.N.A.
A.KRUPA

The final version of the Sant'Agata Bolognese supercar, the LP 780-4 Ultimae, was created to be the definitive Aventador, concluding an era of traditional, naturally aspirated Lamborghini V12s, and was produced in a limited edition of 350 numbered examples of the coupé and 250 of the roadster. In this version, the 6.5-liter (396.65 cu. in.) "Longitudinale Posteriore" V12 was uprated to produce 780 cv (769.47 hp) at 8,500 rpm driving all four wheels, 40 cv more than the Aventador S and 10 cv more than the SVJ (39.46 and 9.87 hp, respectively). The design adopted a specific concept for the front bumpers to increase downforce, with longitudinal performance similar to that of the SVJ.

NEW COUNTACH LPI 800-4

A limited edition produced in 112 examples and paying tribute to the Countach, a maverick icon of revolutionary design and technology on the occasion of its fiftieth anniversary. The Countach LPI 800-4 retains the inimitable experience and sound of the "Longitudinale Posteriore" (LP) V12, combined with the hybrid technology developed for the Sián. The LPI 800-4's V12 power unit delivers 780 cv (769.5 hp), combined with 34 cv (33.5 hp) from the electric motor, for a total of 814 cv (803 hp) (rounded down for the sake of convenience to 800 in the name) through the permanent all-wheel system and can achieve a top speed of 355 kph (220.6 mph), with 0–100 kph (0–62 mph) acceleration in just 2.8 seconds. The Countach's distinctive profile, with its sleek lines running from front to rear, sharp creases, and wedge-shaped configuration innovated the design of modern supercars and future Lamborghini models. The final profile was pure and clean and featured references to the original model, the LP 500, and the LP 400. The Quattrovalvole version of the Countach's inspiration for the LPI 800-4's front end can be seen in the bold lines of the hood, with the long, low, rectangular grille and headlights, and in the wheel arches, with their hexagonal theme. The steeply sloping cockpit silhouette echoed that of the original Countach. The absence of the wing enhanced the purity at the rear, while the air scoops were harmoniously integrated into the car's muscular shoulders, embellished with the Countach's typical louvers.

2021

HURACÁN TECNICA

2022

ON TRACK WITH THE HURACÁN TECNICA

Press a button and your body's frequency changes, tuning into the vibrations and notes emitted by the 5.2-liter (317.3 cu. in.) V10 behind you. There's no shamanic ritual, but the process of firing up the Lamborghini Huracán Tecnica, the latest Sant'Agata supercar, arouses decidedly old-school emotions. Despite being a thorough restyling of the Huracán EVO, itself launched in 2019, the Tecnica is actually the "civilized" version of the Super Trofeo Stradale. In fact, it shares the STO's 640 cv (631.36 hp), rear-wheel drive, four-wheel steering, and painstaking attention to the needle on the scales with a weight-to-power ratio of 2.15 kg/cv (4.815 lbs./hp). Added to this is a setting designed to ensure optimum performance, while at the same time guaranteeing driving comfort suitable for everyday life.

The styling combines the Raging Bull's past and future, starting with the front bumper, with a Y design inspired by the Terzo Millennio concept, the lines of the glazing that follow what has already been seen on the SCV12, and a rear bumper paying tribute to the historic Countach. All this is combined with improved aerodynamics: With respect to the EVO (compared to which it is 6 centimeters [2.36 inches] longer), the Tecnica improves rear-axle downforce by 35 percent and reduces drag by 20 percent. On board we find a connected cabin, where everything is controlled from the large touchscreen compatible with Apple CarPlay, Android Auto, and Amazon Alexa. Mirroring what we have already seen on the STO, the HMI (human-machine interface) includes a telemetry system and on-board logs recording destinations and track times connected to the Unica app.

Now, however, the time has come to do what every enthusiast is eager to do when faced with the Tecnica: drive it. The very moment you press the central button, you have confirmation of that old-school impression. No lithium-ion battery powering the car electrically, no amplifier boosting the exhaust noise, no turbine contributing to increased power. Naturally, this is not to say that the Tecnica is a mechanically dated car; quite the contrary. The Sant'Agata engineers have raised the bar yet again thanks to the recalibrated LDVI (Lamborghini Integrated Vehicle Dynamics) system and the precisely calibrated driving modes—Strada, Sport, and Corsa—with specific suspension settings. In the hills behind Valencia, the Tecnica shows millimetrically precise handling, with a "granitic" front end even when turning up the pace. Traveling in Strada mode, the comfort level is almost GT-like, thanks to the excellent soundproofing and supple absorption of bumps. In Sport mode, things get serious and the car's oversteering character is enhanced, albeit in a way that is always easily managed. We switch to Track mode when we enter the gates of the Ricardo Tormo circuit, where the Tecnica sets the adrenaline coursing and has us smiling at every slide, with the carbon-ceramic braking system never unprepared and guaranteeing consistency and durability. The final verdict? Excellent for having combined the qualities of the STO with greater ease of use—all for the sum of 325,000 euros.

SIÁN FKP 37 LEGO TECHNIC

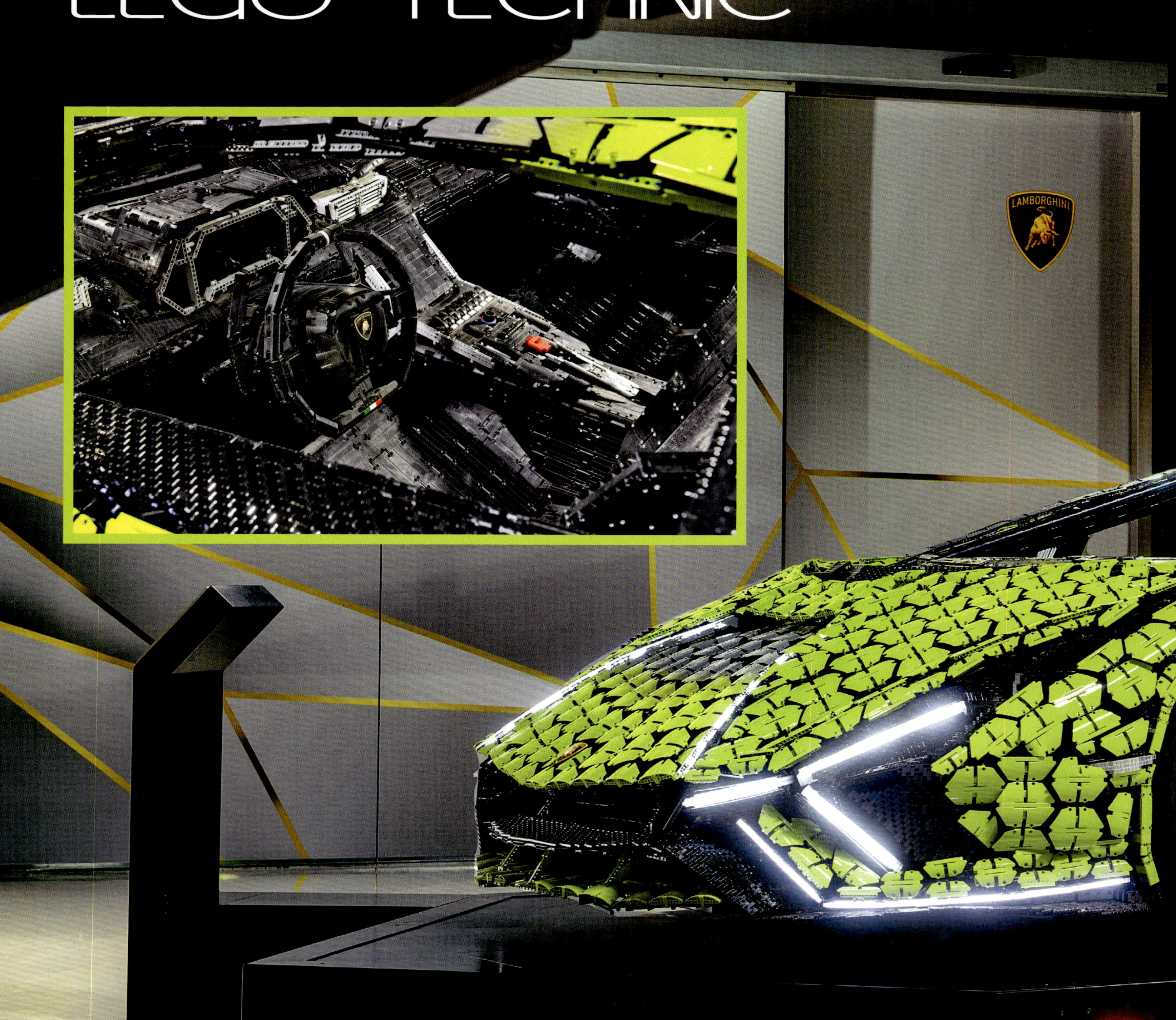

A life-size Lamborghini made of LEGO pieces. Impossible? No. After several months of planning on paper, the supercar replica was created with more than 400,000 LEGO pieces. Overall, the production of the special Sián FKP 37 required 8,660 hours and a team of fifteen people. A total of 154 different LEGO elements were used, of which twenty were created specifically for this model. The final dimensions faithfully reproduced those of the real car, with a length of 4.98 meters (16.3 feet), a width of 2.1 meters (6.9 feet), and a height of 1.13 meters (3.7 feet).

URUS PERFORMANTE

2022

ON TRACK AND OFF-ROAD WITH THE URUS PERFORMANTE

As well as increasing the power to 666 cv (651 hp), they fitted new steel springs, installed a long list of carbon fiber and lightweight components, integrated a torque vectoring system capable of transferring that power to the ground, and implemented a specific calibration of the Torsen center differential, with the Urus Performante adding a Rally mode among those on the so-called Drum control. And it is precisely after selecting this mode that we begin our first test on the Vallelunga off-road track, enjoying ourselves like kids at a funfair as we get over 5 meters of SUV sideways. The performance shown on the off-road track makes us regret the cancellation of the Urus STX project (along with the relative one-make championship with races on asphalt and dirt) but confirms the versatility of the innovative Emilian vehicle. Now, however, it is time to get behind the wheel of a Urus Performante, equipped with Pirelli Trofeo R tires developed specifically for this model on 22-inch forged wheels (23-inch rims are optional) with titanium bolts. And here begins a real inner challenge; on the one hand, your brain reminds you that you are at the wheel of an SUV that is over 5 meters (16.4 feet) long and 2 meters (6.6 feet) wide, but on the other hand, your whole body receives completely different sensations as you tackle the Curvone at speeds befitting a supersports car. The Performante's added value is that it has become even sharper and more reliable than the first-generation Urus, showing such precision in maintaining trajectories that many principles of physics are called into question. In the most technical part, it lifts the inner rear wheel more than once, as if we were at the wheel of a coupé weighing a few hundred kilos rather than a SUV with over 600 liters (over 21 cu. ft.) of loading capacity.

Full marks also go to the carbon-ceramic braking system, a valuable ally in late braking and thoroughly reliable throughout the day on the track, and to the automatic gearbox, capable of varying its character according to the driving mode.

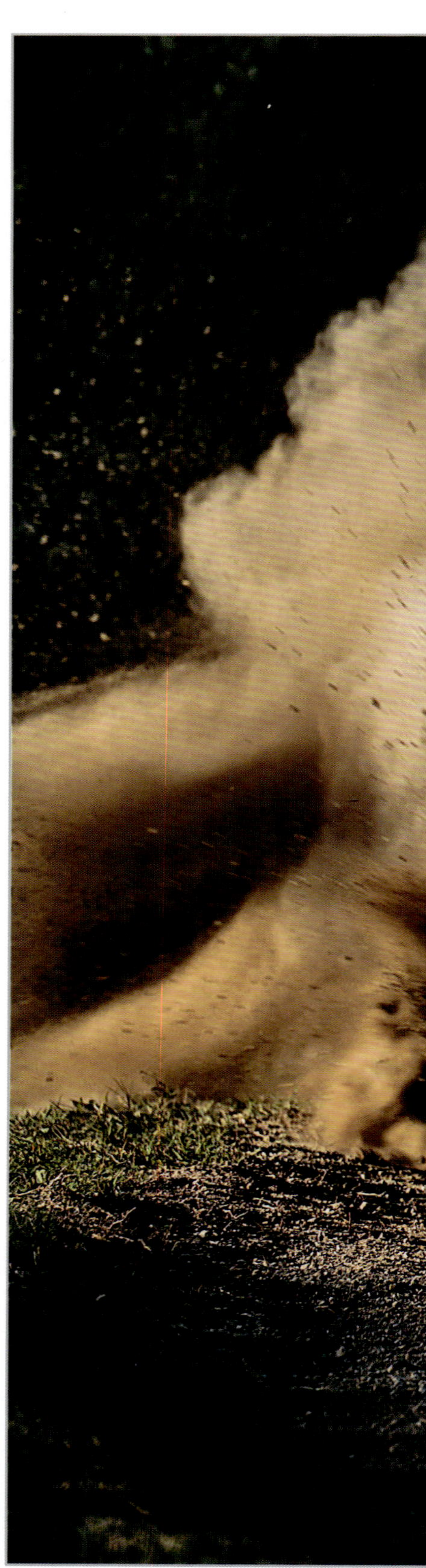

URUS PERFORMANTE

ITALIAN STATE POLICE

The collaboration between Automobili Lamborghini and the Italian State Police began in 2004, with the delivery of the first Gallardo 510-4, which was used for organ transportation. In 2008 the first Gallardos were replaced with the Gallardo LP 560-4. In 2014, Automobili Lamborghini delivered to the State Police a Huracán LP 610-4, followed by a second example in 2017. In February 2023 the Huracán in service with the Emilia-Romagna Highway Police Department was involved in a delicate organ transport operation, helping save the life of a fifty-seven-year-old woman. The latest car to join the State Police fleet is a Urus Performante, delivered in December 2023 and fitted out with a defibrillator, special equipment, and refrigerated storage for organ transport, with a display and data-logger for constant temperature monitoring.

FEDERICO FOSCHINI: THE EVOLUTION OF THE COMPANY

Federico Foschini is the chief marketing and sales officer and a member of the board of Automobili Lamborghini. Born in Ravenna on August 20, 1972, he graduated in engineering management and has been a part of the Lamborghini team for over twenty years. He has held several positions with increasing responsibility, initially in the procurement area and then as project management officer. He was appointed sales and marketing director in 2015 before taking over as chief procurement officer in 2019. Since March 2021, he has been Lamborghini's chief marketing and sales officer.

Your first Lamborghini memory?

I first joined Lamborghini in 1988 as an engineering student, gaining work experience with the company while preparing my thesis and subsequently on a placement. The first "encounter" was with the product, actually touching dream cars. I was then taken on in 1999 and had the opportunity to experience the initial phases of the acquisition by Audi. This was a truly pioneering situation, as the company was coming off the back of difficult years and with an annual production of around 200 cars built by a staff of around 200 people. The first objective was to install the famous group synergy at a procurement level, a situation that meant I was frequently in Germany working with the Audi board and the CEO of the time.

How has Lamborghini changed over the course of your long career?

It's changed radically while always maintaining that passion that has distinguished it since its founding. It has passed from an artisan phase to an industrial phase. While when I set out in my career, Lamborghini was a company with an important history but of modest dimensions and was hardly a thriving economic concern, today everything has changed, starting with the expansion of the factory, the number of employees, the commercial and financial results, and the vision for the future. Going back in time, the birth of the Gallardo confirmed the desire and the possibility of growing and expanding the client base. The first great challenge came with the Aventador, increasing the number of processes associated with procurement and production. With the Urus we tackled the greatest transformation in the history of Lamborghini, achieving our objectives given the results obtained.

What do your clients expect from a Lamborghini?

They expect the transparency, the sincerity, and the respect of our values; that is to say, the creation of cars with extraordinary style and reference performance. All combined with elevated driving pleasure, a renewal of the range, but at the same time a product life cycle that enhances their value. To all this is added an attention to personalization, with the Ad Personam program present on 90 percent of the cars leaving our production lines, confirmation of a desire for unique products.

The sales network continues to expand; what objective have you set?

The sale network is present in 56 markets with 188 dealers, and we are aiming to reach 200 by the end of the decade. Added to this total are the lounges we manage, starting with those in New York and Tokyo, which by the end of 2025 will be joined by those in Miami and Dubai. Along with the addition of around sixty dealers since the launch of the Urus, we have done much to develop the attention paid to the client by the dealers, with a wealth of activities that range from gala evenings to dynamic events on track, on the road, and on snow and ice. The dealers are our ambassadors around the world and will continue to play a key role in our commercial strategy.

HURACÁN STERRATO

UP CLOSE

A coupé capable of supercar performance on and off road. Impossible? No, not if we are talking about the Huracán Sterrato. Compared with the Huracán EVO, from which it was derived, the Sterrato was equipped with an updated version of the Lamborghini Integrated Vehicle Dynamics (LDVI) system, with specific Strada and Sport settings, to which was added the innovative Rally mode dedicated to low-grip situations. It is immediately apparent that an off-road passion animates this limited-edition car produced in just 1,499 examples. The ride height was increased by 44 millimeters (1.73 inches) with respect to the EVO to guarantee greater suspension travel, while the front and rear tracks were widened by 30 and 34 millimeters (1.18 and 1.34 inches), respectively. Moreover, an aluminum skid plate was added at the front, along with reinforced sills, a rear diffuser, and extended wheels arches, all offering protection on loose surfaces.

2022

The air scoop on the rear engine cover ensured that even when tackling dusty routes, clean air would be fed to the 5.2-liter (317.3 cu. in.) V10, producing 610 cv (602 hp) and 560 Nm of torque. The seven-speed gearbox is combined with a dual clutch and electronically managed all-wheel drive, along with a mechanical self-locking rear differential. Capable of sprinting from 0 to 100 kph (0 to 62 mph) in 3.4 seconds, it could achieve an electronically limited maximum speed of 260 kph (161.5 mph). The Sterrato was fitted with ventilated

and drilled 380-millimeter carbon ceramic brake discs and 19-inch wheel rims with Bridgestone Dueler 235/40 tires at the front and 285/40 covers at the rear. The interior, characterized by Sterrato Green Alcantara upholstery, featured a touchscreen with new graphics, Amazon Alexa compatibility, and dedicated loose surface functions. There was also a digital inclinometer with a pitch and roll indicator to measure the car's angles, a compass, and indicators for geographical coordinates and steering angles.

POLO STORICO

CERTIFYING THE LAMBORGHINIS OF THE PAST

The Polo Storico Lamborghini was established in 2015, giving greater value to the existing restoration center; taking responsibility for the management of the historical archives, the car restoration center, and the certification of historic vehicles; and also ensuring the availability of numerous original spare parts related to all historic Lamborghini models. Over the past ten years, the Polo Storico's activities have expanded exponentially, becoming the global benchmark when it comes to Lamborghinis produced up to 2001. Numerous parts have been remanufactured for classic Lamborghinis, with more than 200 new product codes introduced in 2018 alone. Among the most significant certifications was that of the Miura P400, chassis #3586, the original car from the 1969 film *The Italian Job*. The Polo Storico's reconstruction started out from the documentation held in the company's archives and an analysis of the car. The findings were then supplemented with testimonies from enthusiasts and former employees, including Enzo Moruzzi, the stuntman who brought the car to the set and drove it in all the shots.

KUKA

MAURIZIO REGGIANI: FROM THE DIABLO TO THE URUS

Maurizio Reggiani was born in 1959 at Mirandola, in the province of Modena. A car enthusiast from childhood, he attended the Istituto Tecnico G. Galilei, graduating in mechanical engineering. He joined Maserati in 1982, working in the engine design office through 1987, the year in which he left the company to join Bugatti, where, again involved on the design side, he worked on the development of the engine and transmission for the EB110. In 1995, he joined Lamborghini as head of the mechanical engineering department. In 1998, he played an active role in the company's takeover by Audi, and from 2006 to 2022 he was appointed as chief technical officer and a member of the Board of Management. During this period he strengthened the research and development department, expanding the team from 60 to more than 300 people and implementing the most advanced modeling and simulation software systems. In 2023 he was awarded an honorary degree in mechanical engineering by the chancellor of the University of Bologna.

Your first Lamborghini memory?

It would be of a company with an epic past but that found itself in a difficult situation. Walking along the Diablo SE production line, seeing these distinctive colors was something different for an engineer. Seeing this immense spoiler, this stunning engine. I started out from this car to create the Diablo SVR, the first car to be used in a Lamborghini one make championship.

What changed with the arrival of Audi?

Audi changed the way we "approached" the cars. The firm implemented a modus operandi for the creation, construction, and launch of cars that has allowed us to achieve a quality standard that is the envy of the world. To this was added the elevated possibility of investments, of corporate know-how, and greater collaborations with third-party firms. When I arrived in 1995, we were producing around 200 cars a year, built by 200 employees. In 2023, we passed the 10,000-car threshold for the first time.

The most demanding challenges?

The first great challenge was the production of the Aventador. After having become chief technology officer in 2006, the only non-German technical director in the whole of the Volkswagen group, in 2007 I presented an all-new project. The Aventador was based on a design with a carbon fiber chassis, push-rod suspension, and a new V12 engine.

What was the most exciting project?

After the Aventador, without doubt the Urus. No one believed we could do something so different, starting out from one of the group's platforms. Despite my background with "low" cars, having to control roll and pitch was something truly complex from an engineering point of view.

I managed to convince the powers that be to follow my indications regarding four kinds of technical expedients: using a new seat mount on the platform to lower it as much as possible, fitting a mechanical torque vectoring device to improve handling, choosing adaptable torsions bars with adaptive rear steering. A last request concerned the selector for the different driving modes, nicknamed the "tamburo" or drum; it entailed a major investment in economic terms and the time required, but it immediately changed the perception of the interior.

Which three models have remained close to your heart?

The Reventon because it was my first few-off and also the company's. The second is the Sesto Elemento, thanks to its weight of under 1,000 kilos (3,351 lbs.) and a go-kart-like driving precision. The third is the Huracán Performante, with the changes introduced thanks to the active aerodynamics of the ALA (wing) system.

THE AD PERSONAM PROGRAM

Creating one's own car like a true bespoke tailored suit, with a practically infinite range of customization options. This is the concept behind the Ad Personam program, which was introduced in 2006 and has grown year over year with the creation of the dedicated studio in Sant'Agata Bolognese in 2016, which was expanded to an impressive 180 square meters (1,937.5 sq. ft.) in 2023. The renovated spaces provide for a "phygital" experience, connecting the virtual

and real worlds through multiple tools. In fact, customers have the opportunity to fully immerse themselves in the process, involving all their senses, from touch and smell—through the possibility of touching and smelling the upholstery materials—to hearing—listening to the sound of the engine thanks to the uprated sound system—and finally sight—viewing exclusive multimedia materials. The experience begins with a meeting at one of the Lamborghini dealers around the world. Subsequently, the customer is invited to continue the configuration over the course of a dedicated day at the Ad Personam Studio in Sant'Agata Bolognese, exploring endless possible choices and drawing inspiration from a visit to the production lines. The studio allows all the possible options from the Lamborghini range to be showcased in one place, according to increasing levels of customization, ranging from more straightforward configurations, defined as the "Ad Personam essential" range and represented by an expansion of the car's color and trim offerings, to the "One Shot" mode, based on specific customer requests or the use of exclusive, non-automotive materials. Even the design of the studio's interior spaces and the arrangement of materials was conceived by studying and re-creating the optimal configuration process; one of the key elements, in fact, is the choice of color and the treatment of the car's exterior elements, which are extensively displayed as soon as you cross the threshold of the new studio's entrance. Inside, a rotating platform placed in the center of the room allows all the details of the car to be illustrated, even while you are sitting comfortably in the lounge. Body color, wheel rims, brake calipers, logos, exhaust tailpipes, interior upholstery materials such as, but not exclusively, leather, the choice of threads for stitching and embroidery, belts, and interior trim element finishes are just some of the details that can be customized thanks, in part, to the work of the upholstery shop, which combines innovation with tradition and craftsmanship.

2023

MUSEO LAMBORGHINI

PRESERVING THE LEGEND

Established in 2001, the Automobili Lamborghini Museum is a must-see for any enthusiast of the Raging Bull marque. Fully renovated in 2023, it is situated in an important area with a wealth of history. It is, in fact, part of that first nucleus of buildings for which, in 1963, Ferruccio Lamborghini laid the foundation of what would become a company capable of creating an extraordinary history, an authentic source of inspiration for future generations.

The museum presents Lamborghini's enthralling history and iconic models, which along with tours of the production lines illustrate the more than sixty years of innovation that have propelled the marque into the future.

From the first visionary creations of the founder's genius, such as the Miura and Countach, through to the most recent and most exclusive supercars such as the Huracán Performante, the Aventador SVJ, the "few-off" Centenario, the Sesto Elemento, and the Veneno, to the first Lamborghinis with Sián hybrid technology and the Countach LPI 800-4. The Lamborghini Museum offers an interactive experience, thanks in part to the new driving simulator, which amplifies the excitement and enhances your discovery of the cars on display.

Guided tours starting from the museum make your visit an unforgettable experience as you visit some of the company's most surprising places. In fact, it is possible to enter the heart of Automobili Lamborghini and visit the production lines on a unique journey exploring craftsmanship and technology and allowing you to witness the birth of the Sant'Agata Bolognese company's supercars.

2023

REVUELTO

REVUELTO

2023

The Lamborghini Revuelto debuts a completely new hybrid architecture and a new generation of V12 power units, with a lightweight, high-specific-power lithium-ion battery housed in the central portion of the chassis, where on previous generations the transmission tunnel was instead located. The first HPEV (high-performance electrified vehicle) hybrid V12 supercar boasts an impressive 1,015 cv (1,001 hp), power transmitted to the road through an all-wheel-drive system and capable of ensuring a top speed of 350 kph (217.5 mph) and a 0–100 kph (0–62 mph) sprint time of just 2.5 seconds.

INSIDE THE BIRTHPLACE OF THE REVUELTO

"To produce the Revuelto, we realized that we had to go further. This is a hybrid car, very customizable, but at the same time handcrafted. To make it, we raised the bar, creating what we call the 'Manifattura Lamborghini Next Level': a production system that always keeps man at the center but which we adapted to a much more complex product and processes that we did not use before. With the introduction of the Revuelto, we have achieved an expansion of the company's surface area by 172,000 square

meters [1,851,392.59 sq. ft.]," says Ranieri Niccoli, Automobili Lamborghini's chief manufacturing officer. In terms of production, in fact, Lamborghini has embarked on a path that is referred to as manufacturing 4.0. The system that manages the mechanical and technological aspects is known as the MES (manifacturing executive system). This system involves humans who, at every step, are supported by the machine but at any time can interact with it to modify certain activities or stop its operation. The system also manages cobots, collaborative robots that are used on all lines (engines, assembly, and upholstery) in which repetitive actions are required, such as, for example, the fitting of windshields. Playing a leading role in this car is carbon fiber, made with artisanal and automated processes in the CFK plant in Sant'Agata Bolognese. It is the principal structural element of the new car, used to make not only the monocoque chassis but also many of the bodywork elements.

REVUELTO: HOW IT GOES, HOW IT SOUNDS

A concentrate of innovations, technology, and passion. This is the first sensation when you climb aboard the Lamborghini Revuelto, a car capable of providing thrills on track with the symphony played by the V12 engine while also being comfortable and quiet on city streets. Together with the hybrid powerplant, three new dedicated driving modes also make their debuts: Recharge, Hybrid, and Performance, to be combined with the Città, Strada, Sport, and Corsa modes selectable via two rotors on the redesigned steering wheel, for a total of thirteen different experiences according to the circumstances and type of road or track you are driving on. "Città," for example, is the driving mode designed for everyday use in urban areas and even provides for zero emissions. "Strada" is perfectly suited to everyday dynamic driving and long trips, combining elevated comfort with elevated performance, expressing up to 886 cv (874 hp) of maximum power. The V12 is always active, which also guarantees a constant recharging of the battery, which is optimized in Recharge mode. The e-axle supports torque vectoring, and the active aerodynamics deploy to offer maximum stability at high speeds; for example, on the highway. When the "Sport" mode is selected, the character of the Revuelto changes, and the handling and responses of the car are set to offer an emotional "fun to drive" experience in each of the three sub-modes: Recharge, Hybrid, and Performance. The internal combustion engine, assisted by the hybrid system, is active in all three situations, delivering a maximum power output of 907 cv (895 hp), and the sound of the V12 expresses its most captivating tones; the gearbox responds with lightning reactions, while the suspension and aerodynamics exalt the car's agility and the pleasure of driving through corners. The utmost performance and sound are reached with the "Corsa" mode, conceived to exalt the Revuelto's dynamic capabilities on track. With "Performance" selected, the powertrain can express its full potential, reaching a maximum power output of 1,015 cv (1,001 hp); the control system of the hybrid component is calibrated to get the best out of the e-axle in terms of both torque vectoring and all-wheel drive, providing a driving experience that is both sporting and accessible. In "Corsa Recharge" mode, priority can be given to the battery, maximizing its recharging. It is also possible to disengage the ESC to experience the maximum available power without active control system and to enjoy the thrill of full power standing starts thanks to the "launch control" function, activated by keeping the button at the center of the left-hand button pressed.

By framing the QR code with the camera on your smartphone, you will be able to "climb aboard" the Lamborghini Revuelto thanks to a camera car created exclusively for this book. Turn up the volume and listen to the symphony played by the 12-cylinder engine delivering an incredible maximum power output of 1,015 cv (1,001 hp), thanks in part to the presence of three electric motors, and capable of propelling the car to a top speed of 350 kph (217.5 mph) and reaching 100 kph (62 mph) from a standing start in just 2.5 seconds.

RANIERI NICCOLI: HOW LAMBORGHINI PRODUCTION HAS CHANGED

Ranieri Niccoli is the chief manufacturing officer and a member of the board of Automobili Lamborghini. Born in Bologna on November 12, 1968, he graduated in aeronautical engineering from La Sapienza University in Rome in 1995. He began his career with FIAT Automobili, where he held various positions of increasing responsibility in the production sector, eventually becoming the head of assembly at the Mirafiori factory. He then continued his career with Bonfiglioli Riduttori. He has been the chief manufacturing officer at Automobili Lamborghini since 2008, with responsibility for production, logistics, industrial technologies, and infrastructure.

Your first Lamborghini memory?

I first entered the Sant'Agata Bolognese factory in 2007. When I began my career as industrial director in 2008, I remember the original red paving from the 1960s, still conserved in the main entrance. The factory was of modest dimensions, with around 400 people working there to produce around 2,000 examples of the Murciélago and the Gallardo.

How did production change in the first phase of your experience between 2008 and 2015?

The arrival of the Aventador in 2011 and the Huracán in 2014 changed a whole raft of processes. Taking advantage of these new models, we began, on the factory side, to lay the foundations for what would become our subsequent production process, one that is still in operation. Laying foundations means creating the basic processes, the skills, the infrastructure, the technology, and all the logistical aspects, constructing the base layer onto which we could graft a more specific Lamborghini production process. It was a phase of intensive consolidation, which introduced specific skills regarding the production of carbon fiber. With the Aventador, we began to produce the monocoque in-house, an operation previously undertaken externally. We established an initial upholstery department, improving the processes associated with the production of interiors and lending great structure to the sector. In 2015, we managed to deliver 3,245 cars, surpassing the 3,000-vehicles-delivered threshold for the first time.

With the arrival of the Urus, you launched an unprecedented growth in output. What were the principal challenges?

The production of the Urus represented a profound upheaval at both corporate and industrial levels. This was a completely different challenge from diverse points of view, starting with the expansion of the company, with the addition of more than 500 workers over a period of around eighteen months and a doubling of the production volumes. All this was achieved thanks to those "foundations" laid during the preceding period, which led to an industrial process baptized as "Manifattura Lamborghini." All this was created with the aim of progressing from a maximum output of 3,000 to 4,000 cars a year to a company capable of producing SUVs and achieving outputs of more than 10,000 vehicles, as has been the case in recent years. To achieve this result, we have created a different industrial process, introducing concepts of digitalization and automation with the first AGV collaborative robots, while maintaining qualities of craftsmanship and the importance of the human factor that have always distinguished Lamborghini. The arrival of the Urus also led to the painting of the bodies in-house, emphasizing the growth of the plant.

You now have a fully electrified range. How has production changed, and what will change in the future with the arrival of the fourth model?

To arrive at today's fully electrified range, we have worked hard on the training of our staff and on the internal processes, with an evolution with respect to what we did with the Urus. With the all-electric fourth model, there will be further developments, starting with the layout of the factory through to new areas, with challenges similar to the one we faced with the Urus. Not to forget the key role played by our staff, always at the center of the industrial process with their skills, capabilities, and passion.

LANZADOR

THE RAGING BULL'S FIRST EV

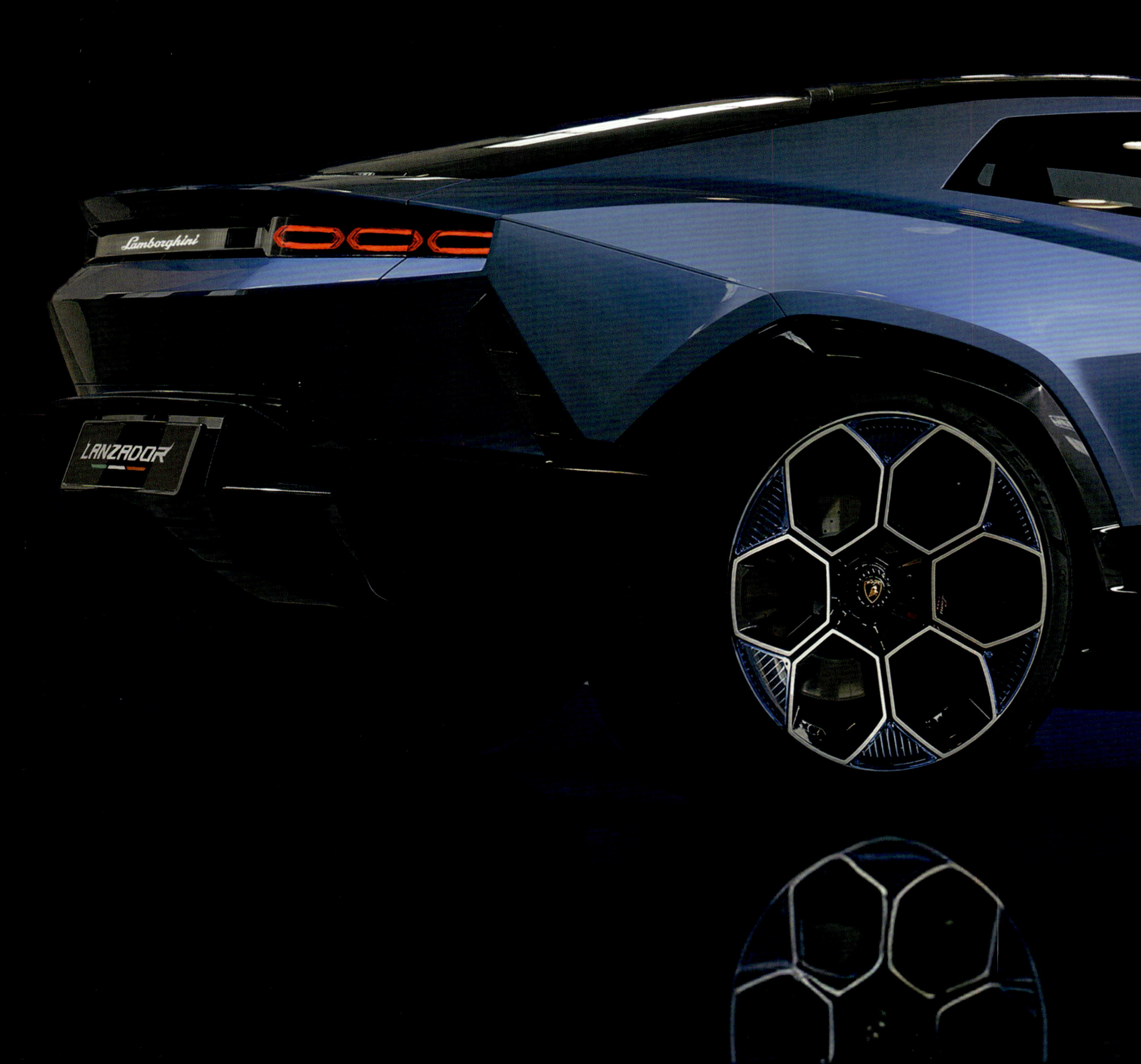

Blasphemy or innovation? The question has to be asked in the face of the first ELIM Lamborghini Lanzador, the first fully electric model produced by the Sant'Agata Bolognese company and presented in 2023. This first model is part of the "Direzione Cor Tauri" strategy, which translates into the decarbonization and electrification path announced in 2021 and anticipates the final version that will arrive in 2028. Characterized by a high-wheel coupé silhouette, the car is equipped with two electric motors, one for each axle, to guarantee all-wheel drive and efficiency in all driving conditions. The Lanzador displays dynamic crossover lines and anticipates styling features to come on the future Huracán.

There's no information on the platform used, but it will most likely be the PPE (premium platform electric) developed by Audi and Porsche. On-board control systems can be adjusted autonomously while driving via controls on the sports steering wheel.

2023

MITJA BORKERT: STYLING SECRETS

Mitja Borkert, born in Germany in 1974, graduated in transportation design from the Pforzheim University of Applied Science in Germany. In 1999, he joined Style Porsche at Weissach, taking on various roles, including that of general manager of advanced design and director of exterior design from 2014. He supervised the development of numerous Porsche models (Panamera Sport Turismo, Porsche Boxster 987 facelift, Cayenne, Macan, and Mission E). In April 2016, he was appointed head of design at Automobili Lamborghini, and since November 2023 he has been design director. Borkert oversees the design of the new models produced by the Raging Bull marque and the coordination of the team of designers. Since joining Lamborghini, he has supervised the creation of models such as the Urus and the Terzo Millennio (2017), the Vision Gran Turismo (2019), the Sián (2019), the Countach LPI 800-4 (2021), the Revuelto (2023), and the Lanzador (2023).

Let's start with your arrival at Lamborghini. Which was the first model you worked on?
The Centenario Roadster, immediately followed by the Aventador S and the Huracán Performante. My first year at Lamborghini was as challenging as it was stimulating.

How does the design of a Lamborghini come about?
We're here to create dreams, to stimulate the senses; we give form to adrenaline. I always stick to the strategy I declared when I joined the company: every Lamborghini must clearly be a "Lambo" and incorporate the DNA of the marque, but it must also have unexpected and innovative elements.

The Revuelto and Temerario have replaced two iconic models such as the Aventador and Huracán. Where did you start out from to achieve the end result?
With the Revuelto, the first high-performance electrified vehicle in the new Lamborghini range, we set ourselves the objective of establishing a new strand in our stylistic language. Even at first sight, the Revuelto reveals itself as an enthralling Lamborghini V12, with taut lines embracing the chassis, celebrating the new exposed powertrain. The Y is the most significant and recognizable signature motif on this new flagship, while the interior represents an emphatic step forward in defining the new direction of Lamborghini design. Every detail of the cockpit communicates our "feel like a pilot" philosophy, which has also been applied to the Temerario. The design of the Temerario is without doubt a new milestone in our stylistic language, which we define as "essential and iconic" thanks to the muscular surfaces and sharp lines that emphasize its proportions and dynamic qualities. Moreover, like the Revuelto, with the Temerario we have again placed the engine stage center, the beating heart of the car and its innovative source of performance.

The fourth model will be all-electric, presenting the Centro Stile with new challenges. What are you working on, and what are the objectives?
The Lanzador is the most visionary and futuristic concept car ever created by Lamborghini, characterized by a surprising design and a new concept of beauty. The proportions are completely new and have been conceived with the intention of inaugurating a new automotive segment. The supercar volumes have been combined with a slightly raised driving position, referencing that of the Huracán Sterrato. It has been conceived for a new generation of digital natives while presenting a new approach to integrating a spacious interior with innovative and sustainable materials. The Lanzador is a brave and unexpected concept car that allows us to visualize today the potential future of the fourth Lamborghini model with its highly emotional character and the new approach to design.

10 YEARS OF LAMBORGHINI SQUADRA CORSE

The Lamborghini Motorsport department celebrated its tenth anniversary in 2023, a decade studded with an impressive list of victories claimed on the most prestigious circuits around the world.

Another milestone was reached by Squadra Corse in 2023, with the tenth edition of the Lamborghini World Finals being held at Vallelunga and achieving record numbers: no fewer than ninety-four cars were entered, arriving from the Super Trofeo Europe, Asia, and North America championships. The environmental sustainability of the event was documented with UNI/ISO 20121:2013 certification.

Since January 2025, Lamborghini Squadra Corse has been directed by Maurizio Leschiutta, the new head of motorsport. Before joining Lamborghini, Leschiutta gained vast experience in the technical and marketing areas of motorsport. After having spent eleven years in Formula 1, focusing in particular on engine development, he turned to GT racing and in recent years has been a key figure in the development of BMW's LMDh program. Among the most important projects he founded on his arrival were the development and management of the SC63 LMDh prototype in its second season in the GTP class of the IMSA series, and the Customer Racing program associated with the Huracán GT3 EVO2, which will be a protagonist in the various international GT championships. The most significant projects for 2025 include the new Temerario GT3, heir to the Huracán GT3.

SQUADRA CORSE

MOTORSPORT: THE HURACÁN ERA AND GT RACING SUCCESS

The Lamborghini Huracán is synonymous with success. Everything started with the Huracán LP 620-2 Super Trofeo, the first racing version of the road-going supercar presented in 2014, which made its track debut in the 2015 season. Produced in 180 examples, this is one of the Raging Bull's winningest models. In parallel with the Huracán LP 620-2 Super Trofeo, in 2015 Lamborghini Squadra Corse presented the Huracán GT3, designed to race in the category of the same name reserved for GT cars. The car's aerodynamics were fine-tuned to provide optimum stability. Just like the Gallardo, the Huracán GT3 won its debut with the Grasser Racing Team, in the first of the five rounds in the 2015 Blancpain GT season. The year 2018 saw the debut of the Huracán Super Trofeo EVO, which raised still further the already elevated standards of the earlier car, thanks to completely redesigned aerodynamics, devices improving safety, and mechanical and electronic novelties. In 2019, it was the turn of the Huracán GT3 EVO, capable of conquering the GT3 category of the principal championships and triumphing in the legendary Daytona 24 Hours. In 2023, Lamborghini took to the track with the third generation of the racing Huracán, the GT3 EVO2, which won the DTM championship title in 2024. For the first time since 1993, an Italian marque and driver conquered the DTM title, with Mirko Bortolotti winning the drivers' championship at Hockenheim in the last race of the season. In Lamborghini's fourth full season in DTM, the second with SSR Performance, the Huracán GT3 EVO2 proved to be one of the most successful cars, claiming a total of nine wins, nine pole positions, and twenty-eight podiums.

2023

LAMBORGHINI ARENA

April 6 and 7, 2024, will go down in the history of Automobili Lamborghini. On these two days, in fact, the first edition of Lamborghini Arena was held at the Imola Autodromo, the event created to celebrate the Sant'Agata Bolognese marque. The event brought together the world of Automobili Lamborghini in one place and time, exalting its passion and successes and celebrating its past and present, always with an eye on the future. In fact, over the two days, visitors could interact with the innovations of the Sant'Agata Bolognese

marque and put themselves to the test by driving, both for real and virtually, the many models that, for the occasion, were available on the Santerno circuit, as well as get in touch with Lamborghini's partners in the various stands in the Autodrome's paddock. More than 6,000 participants and 380 cars, to mention just two of the numbers from the event, which was open to customers, fans, brand enthusiasts, and employees, who, in this way, were able to experience the Lamborghini reality firsthand.

LAMBORGHINI SC63

LAMBORGHINI SC63 DEBUT IN THE LE MANS 24 HOURS

Unveiled in 2023, the Lamborghini SC63 is the first LMDh-class hybrid prototype produced by the Sant'Agata Bolognese-based company. Competing in the Hypercar class of the FIA World Endurance Championship, which includes the 24 Hours of Le Mans, and in the GTP class of the IMSA WeatherTech Sports Car Championship Endurance Cup, featuring classics such as the Daytona 24 Hours and the Sebring 12 Hours, the SC63 is powered by a 3.8-liter (232 cu. in.) twin-turbo V8 engine specially developed by Lamborghini engineers for this car. This unit has a "cold V" configuration, meaning that the turbos are mounted on the outside of the two cylinder banks so that they are easier to cool and feed. In addition, the cold V configuration allows the car's masses and center of gravity to be lowered; this feature, combined with specific balancing and aerodynamic approaches, has been identified as the most effective in achieving the best tire grip, drivability, and consistent speed both in single-lap and long-run race situations. Power output from the internal combustion engine and hybrid system, which is standard for LMDh-class cars, is limited by the regulations to 680 cv (671 hp). The management of the power unit is entrusted to a Bosch electronic control system. The bodywork was designed by the Squadra Corse aerodynamics team in collaboration with the Centro Stile and features unmistakable stylistic elements from contemporary Lamborghini designs, starting with the iconic Y-shaped lights at the front and rear.

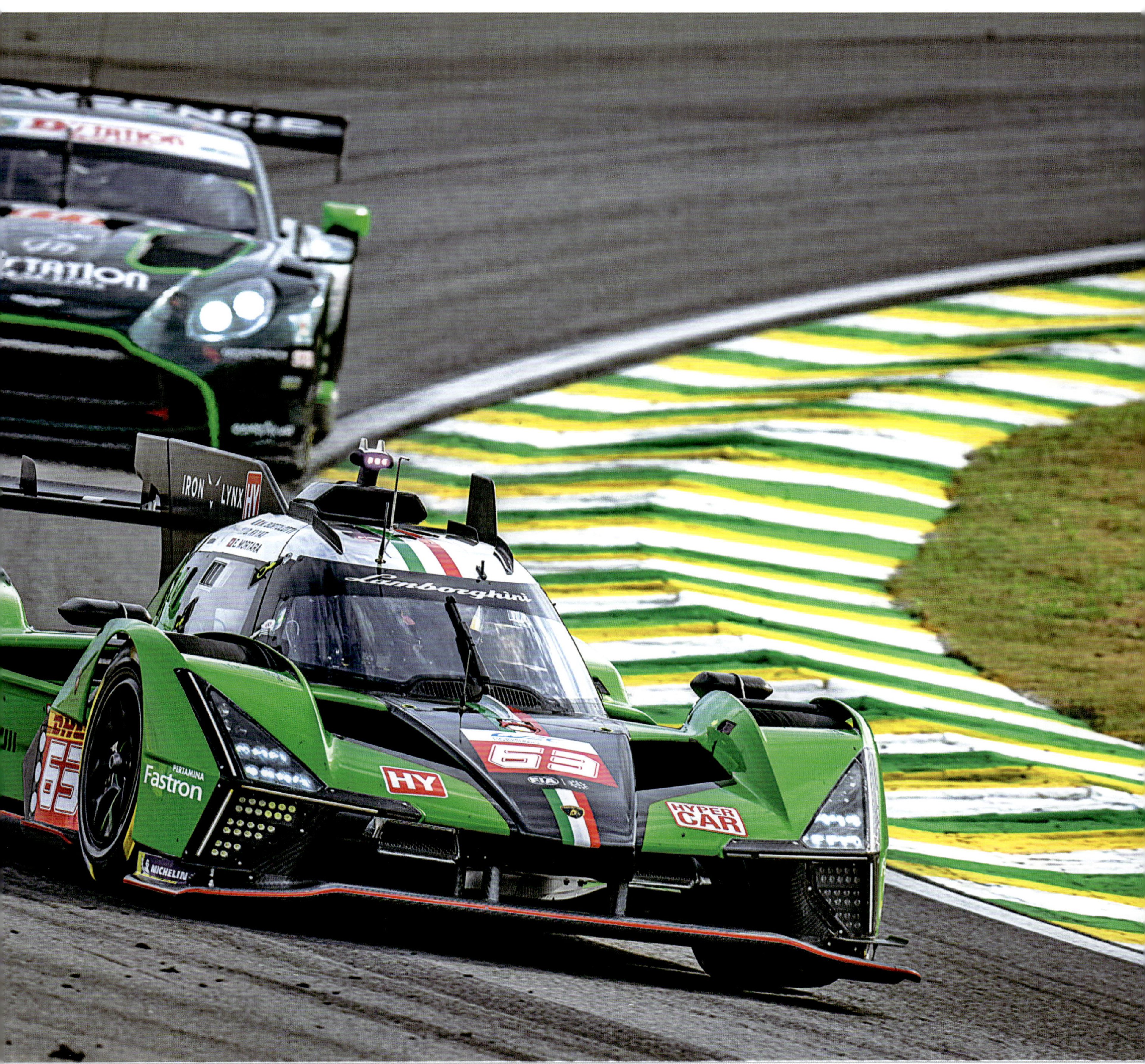

2024

HURACÁN STJ

"THE LAST DANCE"

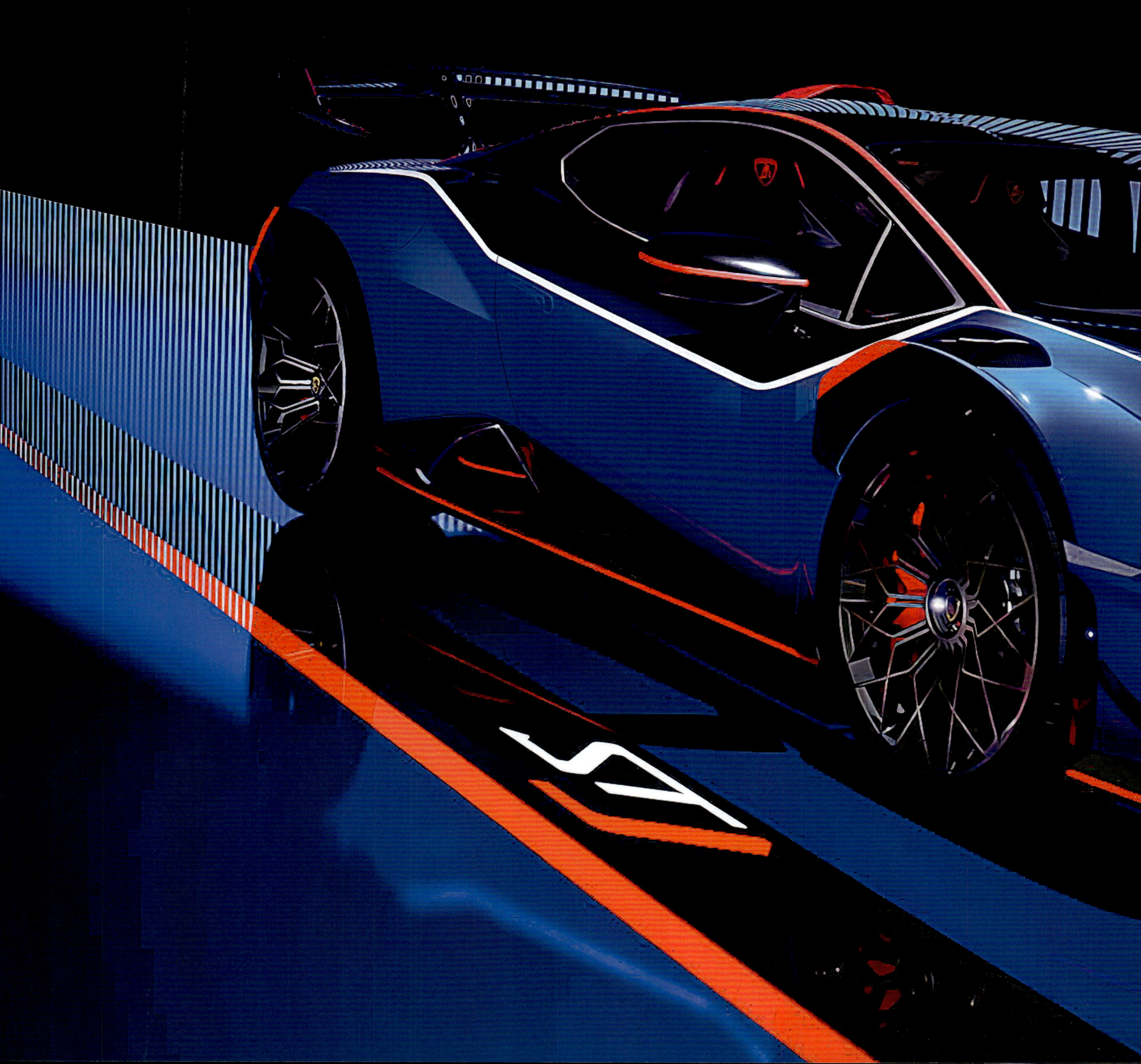

Produced in just ten examples, the Huracán STJ represents the final celebration of the supercar equipped with the naturally aspirated V10 engine. Based on the Huracán STO, the STJ stands for Super Trofeo Jota, with Super Trofeo paying tribute to Lamborghini's one-make racing series inaugurated in 2009 and Jota referencing Annex J of the FIA regulations, which set out the specifications for competition cars and a long tradition of Lamborghini models developed for the track, starting with the Miura SVJ (and continuing with the Aventador SVJ). In styling terms, the STJ is distinguished by a dedicated aerodynamic kit, developed by Lamborghini Squadra Corse engineers on the basis of the know-how gained in ten years at the top in GT racing. The STO's sophisticated aerodynamics have been further refined by adding to the iconic "cofango" hood and fender unit, two all-new aerodynamic appendages (flicks) in carbon fiber. Like the STO, the Huracán STJ delivers a maximum power output of 640 cv (631.36 hp) at 8,000 rpm, developing 565 Nm of torque (at 8,000 rpm) to be handled by the seven-speed LDF (Lamborghini Doppia Frizione, the proprietary dual clutch system) gearbox and exclusively rear-wheel drive.

2024

Lamborghini

URUS SE PLUG-IN HYBRID

Lamborghini Anima
Strada
Sport
Corsa
Sabbia
Terra
Lamborghini
2024

New styling, 800 cv (789 hp), over 60 kilometers of range in electric mode, performance, and a top speed of no less than 312 kph (193 mph). The Lamborghini Urus SE represents the first PHEV (plug-in hybrid electric vehicle) super SUV. The twin-turbocharged 4.0 V8 engine has been reengineered to work in optimal synergy with the electric motor and the 25.9 kWh lithium-ion battery, located below the boot floor and above the electronically controlled rear differential. The permanent magnet synchronous electric motor, upstream of the new eight-speed automatic transmission, can act as a boost for the V8 internal combustion engine but also as a traction element in its own right. Making its debut on the Urus SE is the new central torque splitter with continuous electronic control

and an electro-hydraulically controlled multi-plate clutch; located centrally, it distributes torque variably and continuously between the front and rear axles. The splitter works in synergy with the new electronically controlled self-locking differential installed on the rear axle, making the car oversteer "on demand," conveying the feel of a thoroughbred supercar. The cockpit is designed to highlight Lamborghini's typical "feel like a pilot" DNA and boasts novel features throughout the section of the dashboard in front of the driver, emphasizing that perception of lightness already introduced on the Revuelto. A larger 12.3-inch screen has been installed in the center of the dashboard and features a new human-machine interface.

CARBONFIBER
COFANO:
CARBON FIBER
LAMBORGHINI URUS PERFORMA
* BOLD SPORTINES
* AERODYNAMIC
* LIGHTWEIGHT CO

DOWNFORCE
CIENCY
VENTS
BORKERT
SANT'AGATA BOLOGNESE 2022

NEW
V8 TWIN
TURBO
HYBRID
ENGINE

The V8 engine was designed from scratch at Sant'Agata Bolognese with the aim of delivering performance and driving thrills surpassing even that of the Huracán range, combining the progressive delivery that has been the Lamborghini V10's calling card with the high power and specific torque of a new-generation turbocharged engine. The twin-turbocharged V8 has a displacement of 4.0 liters (244 cu. in.) with a specific power output of 200 hp/liter; the internal combustion engine produces a maximum power output of 800 cv (789 hp) with a maximum engine speed of 10,000 rpm. The rear electric drive system, designed and developed for the new V8 to add an additional 120 cv (118.4 hp), is located between the internal combustion engine and the dual-clutch transmission and includes the inverter as well as the axial-type electric motor.

2024

countach

ROUVEN MOHR: THE BIRTH OF THE NEW V8

Rouven Mohr was born in 1979 at Saarbrücken in Germany. After graduating in engineering from the Technical University of Kaiserslautern and completing a PhD in computational mechanics, he joined Audi in 2008 as a testing engineer for chassis durability in the technical management team. He acquired increasing responsibility and in 2014 was appointed head of project management whole vehicle for the Audi A3, TT, Q7, and Q8 models. In 2017, he moved to Lamborghini, where for two years as head of whole vehicle development he supervised development of the Aventador, Huracán, and Urus before rejoining Audi as head of energy and weight management. In 2020, he was appointed head of verification/validation whole vehicle before returning to Lamborghini as head of the research and development department.

How did the idea of a hybrid twin-turbo V8 for the Temerario come about? What were the most complex challenges?

We wanted to develop a peerless, high-performance sporting power unit that would combine the best of two worlds: that of the internal combustion engine, with a twin-turbo V8, and that of electrification, installing three electric motors to obtain instantaneous acceleration, torque vectoring, and efficient energy recovery. With the Temerario we are redefining the segment; it's a true thoroughbred in terms of both engineering features and performance.

What is the most complex challenge for Lamborghini's chief technical officer in an era of energy and technological transition?

Rather than a limit, hybrid technology represents an opportunity that projects supercars toward a new phase in terms of dynamics and driving experience. This is the dawn of a new era for supercars, in which we are redefining the concept of sportiness, fun, and driving dynamics in the key of sustainability. Our company DNA continues to be based on the concept of emotional performance. It's on these new perspectives that the Research and Development department is focusing its attention, with the goal of bringing the "feel like a pilot" experience to a new level through the continuous development of six fundamental pillars necessary if we are to tackle the challenge of electric cars to best effect: a human-machine interface with "versatility" models such as the Urus, the use of carbon fiber to reduce overall weight, an electric powertrain, an advanced chassis, intelligent aerodynamics allowing even higher performance with respect to current cars to be obtained, and lastly, integrated management offering a driving sensation similar to that of a pilot.

The Lanzador anticipates the fourth model with an all-electric powertrain. What will the first electric Lamborghini be like?

In the future, Lamborghini will differentiate through a different strategy concerning all the active control systems. We're taking the control of vehicle dynamics to a whole new level, offering our clients an absolutely innovative experience: finding the right balance between power, performance, range, and aerodynamics is certainly one of the greatest challenges we'll face during development, but the very concept of a challenge is a Lamborghini cornerstone.

TEMERARIO

2024

UP CLOSE

Presented in August 2024 at Pebble Beach during the Monterey Car Week, the Temerario is aiming to surpass the success of the Huracán thanks to truly outstanding performance. The new hybrid powertrain brings together a new twin-turbo V8 engine and three electric motors for a total power output of 920 cv (907.5 hp). The twin-turbo V8 was designed and developed from scratch at Sant'Agata Bolognese and is the first and only unit in the production supercar category capable of reaching 10,000 rpm. The Temerario is the second model in the Lamborghini HPEV (high-performance electrified vehicle) range after the Revuelto and completes the electrification of the Sant'Agata Bolognese range following the launch of the Urus SE. At 4.71 meters (15.5 feet) long, 2 meters (6.6 feet) wide, and 1.2 meters (4 feet) high, with a wheel base of 2.66 meters (8.7 feet), the Temerario has a cockpit offering adequate space for two people, thanks to the layout of the new chassis and the compactness of

the twin-turbo V8. Making its debut is the new human-machine interface, the car's control and information center. Furthermore, for the first time, the Temerario has been equipped with the optional Lamborghini Vision Unit, offering a full racing driver experience thanks to three cameras and a dedicated control unit with Telemetry 2.0, Memories Recorder, and Dash Cam functions. All this is visible through the 12.3-inch instrument display and the vertical 8.4-inch connected infotainment screen, together with a third 9.1-inch screen in front of the passenger. The applications are easily accessible through the infotainment system and the steering wheel controls, as well as via the Lamborghini Unica app.

The Temerario is also the first Lamborghini immediately available with the Alleggerita (lightweight) package, aimed in particular at those who intend to take the car on track. Thanks to a series of measure, the package trims 25 kilos (55 lbs.) from the car's original weight of 1,690 kilos (3,725.8 lbs.).

Lamborghini
TEMERARIO

By framing the QR code with the camera on your smartphone, you will be able to "climb aboard" the Lamborghini Temerario thanks to a camera car created exclusively for this book. Turn up the volume and listen to the symphony played by the twin-turbo V8 and three 150 cv (148 hp) electric motors developing a total of 920 cv (907.5 hp) and capable of propelling the car to a top speed of 343 kph (213 mph) and reaching 100 kph (62 mph) from a standing start in just 2.7 seconds.

THE AUTHOR

Simonluca Pini was in born in Bologna, at the heart of Motor Valley, in 1982. From a very young age, his passion for cars was overwhelming, a passion that transformed into a profession after completing his studies, when he began contributing to various publications before arriving at *Sole 24 Ore*, Italy's leading economic periodical, in 2016. In a collaboration lasting almost ten years, he attended more than 500 product launches, driving automobiles of all kinds throughout the world, from prototypes to racing cars, and visiting the leading manufacturing facilities, styling centers, and research and development departments. As well as writing for the motor pages, he also contributed to the finance and economy desks, where he was responsible for in-depth studies of issues associated with mobility and the leading figures of the automotive world.

PHOTO CREDITS

All images are provided by Automobili Lamborghini S.p.A.

AUTOMOBILI
LAMBORGHINI

EDITORIAL PROJECT
CONSULTING D&D/VALERIA MANFERTO DE FABIANIS

EDITORIAL COORDINATION
GIORGIO FERRERO

GRAPHIC PROJECT
MARIA CUCCHI

Piazzale Luigi Cadorna, 6
20123 Milan, Italy
www.whitestar.it

Translation: Neil Frazer Davenport – Editing: Andrea Modica

1 2 3 4 5 6 29 28 27 26 25

Published by Schiffer Publishing, Ltd.
4880 Lower Valley Road
Atglen, PA 19310
Phone: (610) 593-1777; Fax: (610) 593-2002
Email: info@schifferbooks.com
Web: www.schifferbooks.com

ISBN 978-0-7643-7041-0

Printed in China
Cover graphic design: Chiara Rizzolo